Mastering
Hand Tool
Techniques

Mastering Hand Tool Techniques

*A comprehensive guide
on how to sharpen, tune and use
classic hand tools to add power
to your woodworking*

ALAN & GILL BRIDGEWATER

Quantum
Books

A QUANTUM BOOK

This book is produced by
Quantum Publishing Ltd.
6 Blundell Street
London N7 9BH

Copyright © MCMXCVII
Quarto Inc

This edition printed 2004

ISBN 1-86160-988-4

QUMMHT

Printed in Singapore
by Star Standard Industries Pte. Ltd

*We would like to dedicate this book to… …
"Marshall & Son – Woodworkers",
to Neil Marshall, his father David, and his
grandfather Harold.*

*We would like to thank Neil Marshall and his
friend and employee Laurence Buttery – two
really good woodworkers – for all their help and
expertise.
Laurence left school way back in the forties,
served his apprenticeship with Neil's father
David, and has worked alongside the family ever
since. Just think about it…fifty years in the same
job and still going strong – that's a lot of stamina,
and loyalty, and know-how, and shaving !*

Contents

Introduction

Wood is a uniquely beautiful material – the stuff that dreams are made of! Of all the gifts of nature, trees are the most wondrous. The air we breathe, our homes, our furniture, our medicines, just about everything about us, is made possible by trees.

Sometimes when I'm alone in my workshop, I run my hands over a piece of wood – one of my carvings, or maybe a surface that has just been planed, or perhaps one of those pieces of plum that I've been saving for I don't know what. It's an incredible feeling: the colour of the wood, the smell, the textures. Every single piece of woodwork is unique, every single board is full of promise, every single project is a lesson learned. And then again, I sometimes take one or other of my woodworking planes and marvel at its weight and form – the exquisite way the steel, the brass and the wood fit, slot and slide together. When I test the keenness of the cutting iron against the pad of my thumb and then go on to lift a crisp clean curl of wood, the feeling is pure pleasure.

This book involves sharing with you the joy of working with wood. These pages are about the hands-on satisfaction of learning by doing, of understanding how and why the tools do what they do. Woodworking is about the unique coming together of wood and tools. Once you understand about the nature of wood, once you understand about the anatomy of the tools – how they are maintained, tuned and held – then the rest will follow.

ABOVE: Medieval woodworker using a ripsaw and a saw–horse.

Is wood just a material that can be bullied into shape? Is woodwork just about getting the job done with maximum speed and efficiency? Are tools just lifeless lumps of wood and steel that are used to force the wood into shape? Are the techniques simply that sum total of a great heap of facts and figures? Well, of course, the answer is no! Certainly you can smash a piece of wood into shape, and you can use and abuse tools and then throw them away, and you can do everything at a fast and furious rate, but where is the pleasure? Where will you be at the end of it all?

This book is about learning by doing, about pleasure by doing. Don't get me wrong, I'm not advocating that you spend your time drifting about the workshop with a lily in one hand and a sonnet in the other. I'm simply saying that the way into the fine art of woodwork – the only way to really understand the techniques – is to spend time finding out how the tools and the wood come together. So, for example, the only way to learn about the technique of using a hand plane is to select a plane and play around with it until you know just about everything there is to know about its shape, form and function. Then select a choice piece of wood and try planing it. You will soon find out why a piece of rough knotty wood is useless and why one plane cuts better than another.

The intention throughout this book is to demonstrate in depth the fundamental truth that traditional woodworking techniques start and finish with the tools. Gill and I guide the beginner into the craft by what we consider is the most logical route. We start by looking at the work area – the bench, lighting and storage. Then we present a guide to the nature of wood, and next, just as an apprentice would have learned the craft, we take you through the logical stages of getting deeper and deeper into the wood. We work through the marking-out techniques, and then we go through the sawing techniques, and then on to planing and so on through the book, all the while getting more involved with the wood.

Along the way, there are step-by-step, hands-on tool workouts that gently introduce you to very specific hand tool techniques and skills. The idea is that once you have mastered the fundamentals of the wood and the tools, then you can go forward and try your hand at the techniques.

An exciting journey into the wonderful world of sawing, carving, turning and joinery, an in-depth look at woodworking traditions, a guide to collecting, tuning and using your tools. This book is all of that and then some!

ABOVE: Wooden smoothing plane – the perfect tool if you can have only one plane, it is versatile and easy to use.

Workshop

Woodworking is a wonderfully rewarding and therapeutic activity, but only if the workshop is safe, comfortable and well organized – with all the tools close to hand. You might be limited to working in the garage, or maybe working in a small shed in the garden, and that's fine, but it's only going to work if there is a place for everything and everything is in its place. Just remember you and the tools are one on this – you both need a working area that is dry, well-lit, dust-free, clean and comfortable.

THE WORKBENCH AND VICE

ABOVE: A classic workbench – with a tail vice and a vice screw – a bench designed for home woodworking.

The workbench is the focal point of the workshop. The bench is where it all happens: the measuring, the planing, the joinery and just about all the other activities. And of course, each and every woodworker has his or her own views as to the perfect bench. Some prefer a small, neat bench with a tool well running down the centre. Others like a huge bench with a flat top – there are as many ideas on the perfect bench set-up as there are woodworkers.

All that said, all woodworkers would agree on certain points: a bench must have a sturdy frame – no shake, wobble, rack or creep. The surface must be firm and at a comfortable height – no springiness, no stooping or reaching. And the structure must allow room for the vice, the dogs, the stops, and all the other pieces of equipment that go to make up the perfect bench.

It might not be possible to please everyone, but at the very least, there is universal agreement that the legs need to be at about 8.75 cm² (3½ x 3½-ins square) – if not larger – and all the other members need to be approaching the 7.6 cm x 6.35 cm (3 x 3-in, or 3 x 2¾-in) mark.

Fitting the Vice

Choose the biggest, best quality vice you can afford – preferably one that is several sizes up on your reckonings. And don't forget to allow for the wood faces that reduce the total opening width. You must also make decisions as to whether or not the wooden face of the inside jaw will stand proud of the front edge of the bench and the front edge of the front face of the vice. Most woodworkers prefer to have both faces of the vice fitted with hardwood cheeks, with all top edges running flush with the top of the bench. But some woodworkers prefer to have the vice fitted with a face board that runs the full length of the bench. Such a board is good for fitting additional stops, clamps and dogs. However, if you do choose this option, then you must be aware that the necessary 3.10 cm x 3.80 cm (1¼–1½-ins) thickness

of the board reduces the capacity of the vice opening.

No matter which of the various vices you fit to your bench, you will almost certainly require packing pieces between the underside of the bench and the vice. The vice will need to be mounted with nuts and bolts, or at the very least with coach screws. If you use bolts, then they are best mounted through the top of the bench, with the bolt heads recessed. Many woodworkers like to glue plugs in the recessed bolt holes and plane them flush to a good finish, but others figure it's a good idea to leave the recesses open. That way, when the time comes for the vice to be replaced or relocated, the bolts will be easily accessible.

- Use only good quality hardwood for the vice faces.
- All screws and bolts should be well below the surface of the wood.
- Follow the manufacturer's advice for mounting and use.
- Get help lifting and mounting the vice.

ABOVE: A lightweight, low-cost vice.

TIPS BOX

A vice is a big investment, but it might well be used daily over twenty or thirty years. Therfore, it pays to get the very best that you can afford. Most woodworkers offer the same two key bits of advice: get a bigger vice than you think you'll need; and if you are short of cash try to find a big second-hand model rather than settling for a smaller new one.

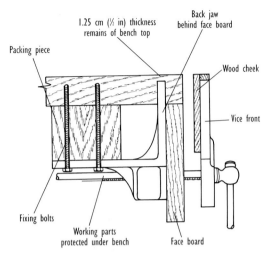

ABOVE: Large vice fixed by coach screws.

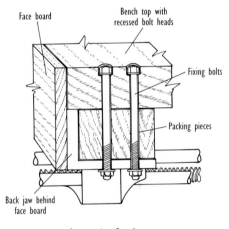

ABOVE: Large vice fixed by countersunk coach bolts.

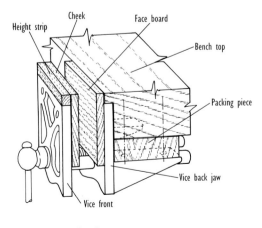

ABOVE: Small vice fixed with screws.

LIGHTING

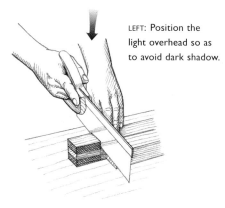

LEFT: Position the light overhead so as to avoid dark shadow.

All work areas should be positioned so that there is an adequate, well-balanced mix of natural light – from windows and top glazed doors – and artificial light from electric ceiling lights, wall lights and portable lamps. The overall aim must always be to have adequate lighting without hard shadows or glare. In a home workshop, most woodworkers prefer to work in front of a window, with a fixed light at top centre, and with the option of using a swing-arm lamp if conditions require.

The key to successful shop lighting is flexibility. The difficulty is that certain specific tasks require specific lighting options. For example, working at the lathe requires an overhead light to illuminate the whole area, and an additional directional light – usually coming in at the side – to shine onto the point of cut. Sometimes, such as when you are turning or drilling hollows, it may be helpful to have an additional light that can be precisely positioned to the interior of the work. Most important of all, from one task to another, and taking into account left-and right-handedness, lighting set-ups should be versatile enough to be relocated to suit changing needs. Of course, if the workshop is big enough, you can move around the bench so that the workpiece is always lit to best effect. But most woodworkers must work at a bench with a single vice with a minimum of all-round space.

As to the question of whether or not to have fluorescent lighting, certainly such lighting is wonderfully efficient and economical. However, there are wood-workers who claim that the flicker is variously a distraction and/or gives them headaches. If you consider this to be a problem, then either stay with conventional lighting, or search out non-flickering alternatives. Either way, for maximum safety you should protect all lights within a wire mesh or cage.

Portable Lighting

A good lighting option is to have one or more portable lights either flex-arm lamps, and/or clip-on-lamps. The flex-arm lamp is particularly useful in that it can first be placed so that it is more or less in the correct position, and then it can be fine tuned so that the light is centred on the area of interest. Once again, you must have the light head protected from bits of flying wood and the like, and you must make sure that the flexible shaft is kept well clear of cutting edges.

Lighting the Workpiece

Many woodworking techniques specifically use light as an aid. For example, saw sharpening requires that light be directed so that it bounces off the bevel of the teeth. Marking out with a pencil and square requires that the light come from the same side as the pencil hand. Chopping a mortise requires that the light illuminates the front of the blade where the wood is being cut. If you are new to woodworking, it is a good idea to plan your workshop initially so that there is a minimum of fixed light sources, and then you can add extra lighting when you more fully understand your needs.

TIPS BOX

Don't be tempted to set up work surfaces and wall lights all around the edge of the room just because it looks neat and tidy on paper. It's much better to start with a main bench set up in front of the window and to build additional small, island work surfaces, adding more lights as you go.

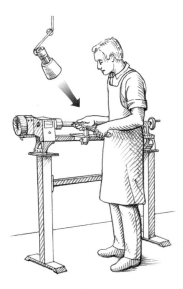

ABOVE: Position the light so that it illuminates the area of interest.

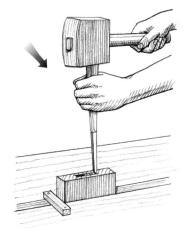

ABOVE: The blade-to-wood area needs to be free from shadow.

STORAGE

Just like people, tools need to be kept dry, warm and comfortable – no damp, no dust, no careless handling. The size, shape and structure of your workshop, as well as the shape and number of your tools, will affect the way the tools should be stored, but the overall needs will be the same. The tools need to be kept dry. They need ideally to be kept apart – so that the blades and edges do not clink against each other. And they need to be organized so that they are close at hand. Options include chests and boxes with trays and compartments; wall cupboards and shelves with hooks and racks; or drawers with compartments and tool rolls. Each has advantages and disadvantages.

Storing Planes

Whether or not your planes are stored on shelves, in cupboards, boxes or whatever, the main need is to protect the blades from impact and abrasion damage. To this end, planes should always be set side-down between tasks. So when you quit planing to answer the phone or have a cup of coffee, then all you do is lay the plane down on its side. As to how to store the tool between jobs, some woodworkers leave the plane on its side, while others claim that it's best to release the cap lock and withdraw the cutter iron, then set the plane flat-down on its sole.

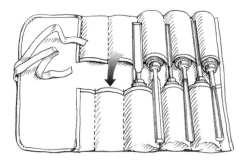

ABOVE: Arrange the tools so that the cutting edges are on view.

Tool Roll

Chisels and gouges are best stored in a tool roll. Though there are many designs, the best option is a roll that allows the chisels and gouges to be slid into pockets. In this way, the tools are contained, and the cutting edges are in full view, so that the woodworker is able to swiftly see what's available. Remember that it's nonsense to have your set of gouges so well contained and hidden that you can't swiftly select the correct tool for the job.

Tool Chest

Traditionally the woodworker's first job when he had attained sufficient skill was to build two tool chests – a large chest with sliding trays and compartments for his main tool storage, and a smaller more portable box for outside jobs. Most of these traditional chests have a deep lift-up lid with storage for T-squares and/or winding sticks, sliding trays for small tools like bevels and squares, drawers with little compartments for the chisels and gouges, and clips and turn-buckles for holding the saws.

Tool chests are a wonderful idea on two counts: The woodworker is able to spend time designing and building an item that is by its very nature a skill-testing challenge, and better yet, it is the best way of ensuring that a tool collection is stored, protected and shown to best advantage. This means, if the tool collection is heavy on planes, or gouges, or woodturning tools, or whatever, then the woodworker can tailor the size and shape of the chest to suit.

ABOVE: If you want to keep your tools safe and dry, then you can't do better than store them in a chest.

Working with Wood

Part of the joy and adventure of working with wood is the fact that no two boards – even from the same tree – are exactly the same. That means the piece of wood you selected might well have cost a great deal of money, and it might look and smell good, and the specialist at the lumberyard might have described it as top quality. But for all that, there is no saying that once the wood is opened, that it won't reveal a flaw that renders it totally useless! The best a woodworker can do, is to minimize the risk of selecting a problem piece of wood by being aware of species characteristics, by learning about such things as grain, texture and figure, and by looking out for symptoms that suggest that the wood is flawed.

GRAIN AND FIGURE

Though strictly speaking the term "grain" has to do with longitudinal growth of the tree, the term has now generally come to mean the pattern of wood fibres that we recognize in the planed wood. A plank might be described as being close grained or coarse grained. Limewood has a straight, smooth, close grain, while oak tends to have a grain that is coarse and wavy. While there are all manner of grain features that are inherent to species – straight grain, spiral grain, wavy grain and curly grain – there are three primary grain characteristics that affect the workability of wood: close grain, coarse grain and cross or diagonal grain.

Close grain results when the growth rate of the tree was even and slow. A cross section through the trunk will reveal that the rings are thin and packed tightly.

Coarse grained wood generally comes from fast-growing trees. A slice through will show a section of loosely packed rings, with irregular spacing. Such a wood tends to be difficult to work. Cross and diagonal grain result when the fibres of the wood are badly aligned and generally awry. This usually makes it difficult to work, although the resulting piece may look spectacular.

Figure

The term "figure" refers to most of the characteristics that mark one species as being different visually from another. The variations in colour and pattern that we see in the milled boards, the knots, decay textures, the grain patterns that are enhanced by various sawing techniques, are known as figure. The character and quality

of the figure does, to a great extent, depend on the natural characteristics of the species, and the way the wood is milled. Some of the most beautiful and prized figure wood is obtained from plain sawing the crotch, and through abnormalities like burls and knots.

Grain Texture

Although the term "texture" refers primarily to the size of the cells within the wood – for the average woodworker it has come to mean the texture of the grain as it affects workability and finish. From the woodworker's viewpoint, a smooth-grained texture is smooth to the touch and shiny to the eye, while an open grained texture is rough to the touch and matt to the eye.

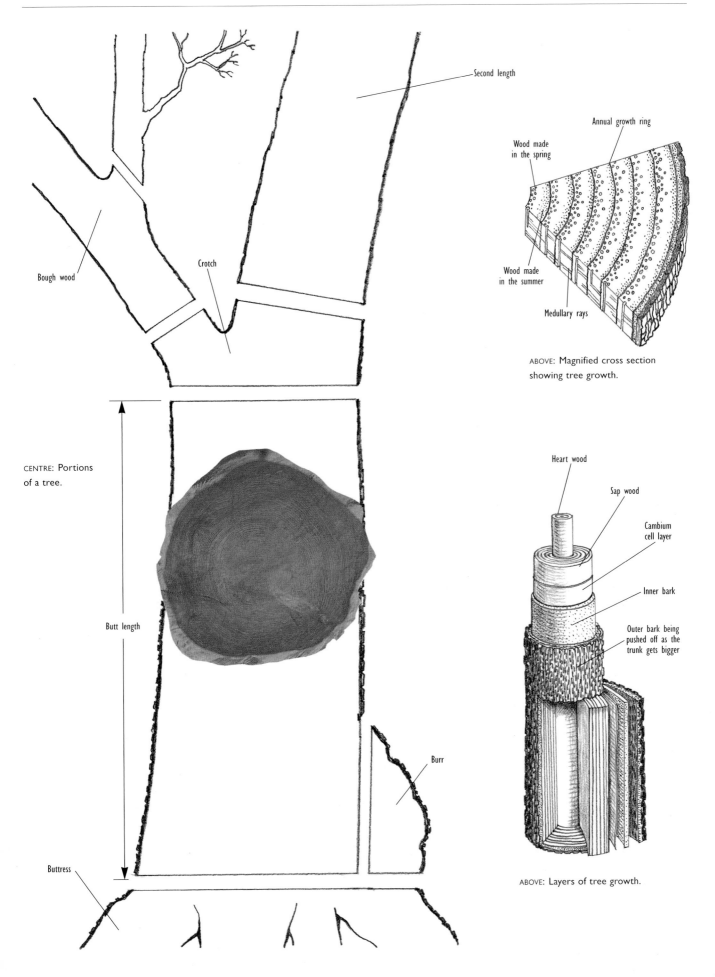

Second length

Annual growth ring

Wood made
in the spring

Wood made
in the summer

Medullary rays

ABOVE: Magnified cross section
showing tree growth.

Bough wood

Crotch

CENTRE: Portions
of a tree.

Butt length

Heart wood

Sap wood

Cambium
cell layer

Inner bark

Outer bark being
pushed off as the
trunk gets bigger

Burr

Buttress

ABOVE: Layers of tree growth.

MILLING WOOD

The size, shape and the grain pattern of the wood that the woodworker gets to use in his workshop is, to a great extent, determined by the way the tree is sliced up or milled. There are many traditional ways of milling lumber: The log can be plain sawn to make a stack of planks, or it can be cut radially into quarters, and so on. Sometimes a single large-diameter log is first quartered, and then each quarter is sawn in a different way. The diagrammatic illustration below shows four methods of milling a quartered log.

Radial Sawing

Also called quarter-sawing, this is a method of sawing roughly parallel to the medullary rays with the result that the figure rays appear on the face of every board. Certainly the radial cut produces the best boards for overall dimensional stability, but against this, there is a great deal of waste. This method is only used for high quality work when a choice figure is desired.

RIGHT: Four different methods of quartering timber.

Medullary Cut

Also called rift-sawing, this method is a compromise between the more wasteful radial cut and the efficient thick plank cut. Though this a good method of obtaining all-figured wood, it is more complicated and more expensive, and the dimensions of the resulting boards are necessarily less.

Thick Plank Cut

This method gives thick planks with the minimum of waste. It is primarily a way of obtaining a mix of choice boards and ordinary structural lumber.

Plain Saw

Ordinary planks are described as being plain sawn, or you might say they are sawn through-and-through, or even slash sawn. Though we show a quarter being sawn in this way, it is more usual to run the whole trunk through so as to produce 3 inch or smaller planks, with the middle-of-stack planks being the full width of the trunk. Certainly this is the easiest and the most economical way of milling lumber, and it is good for low grade wood. Although it does produce the widest boards, some of the boards are unstable, depending upon the position of the planks in the stack. Thus, there a big difference in the handling characteristics and in the figure of the individual boards. When a whole log is plain sawn, the boards at the top and bottom of the stack are the narrowest with almost no figure, and then successive boards show more and more figure until they approach the half-way mark across the diameter. Or to put it another way, the majority of the boards show the minimum of figure, hence the term plain.

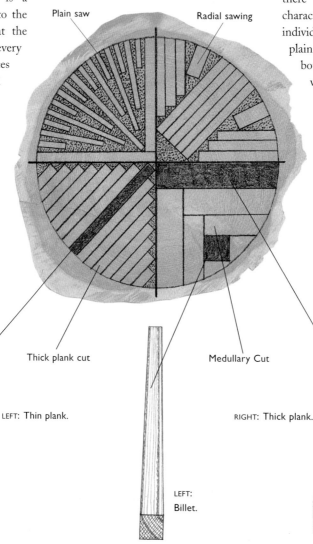

Plain saw   Radial sawing

Thick plank cut   Medullary Cut

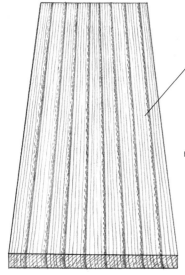

LEFT: Thin plank.

LEFT: Billet.

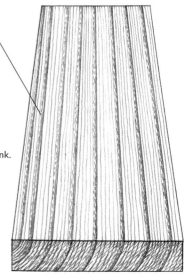

RIGHT: Thick plank.

DEFECTS TO AVOID

In the terms of this book, defects are classified as being either natural defects related to the tree's growth, such as disease and decay, and artificial defects that may relate to the way the wood has been cut and/or seasoned.

Decay

Although decay, such as rot and mould, does sometimes result in the wood being unusually coloured or patterned, as in spalted wood, it is for the most part an indication that the wood is unusable. Best to avoid wood that in any way shows evidence of decay.

Insect Attack

Insect pests can dramatically reduce the structural integrity of a piece of wood. Small neat holes may indicate that the pest has come and gone, but for all that, a piece of wood that shows insect holes is best avoided.

Cup Checking

Splits or checks that occur towards the middle of the tree around the pith are termed cup checks or shakes. The defect isn't serious in the sense that it is evidence of decay or whatever, but rather it does render the piece of wood less than perfect.

Star Checking

Usually the result of rushed seasoning and consequent rapid shrinking, star-checked wood is best avoided if for no other reason than that the end that shows the checking has to be sawn off and wasted.

Heart Checking

Heart checks are a really good indicator that the growing tree was old and shrinking from the heart. The end that shows the checks needs to be cut away; who knows how far the split runs up the wood?

Round Checks

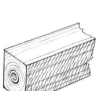

Round checks or ring checks at the pith of the tree seriously affect that value of the wood as they suggest that the growing tree was excessively old and/or that the growing tree was put under intense stress, such as heat, wind or flood. Such wood is best avoided.

Through Checking

A check that extends from one surface through to another – caused by stress and/or old-age shrinkage – usually renders the wood useless.

Splits

Splits result when wood cells are torn apart. They are usually caused by careless seasoning such as too rapid drying.

Loose Knots

Loose or unsound knots suggest that some part of the wood is in an advanced state of decay. The problem is, of course, that loose knots are liable to fall out when the wood is used.

Wany Edge

An edge of plank that shows bark is soft and generally unusable. Be mindful that when you buy board widths that show bark on a wany edge, the bark will need to be cut away, resulting in narrower boards.

ABOVE: Movement in planks of wood, from left to right: springing, bowing, winding and cupping.

STRENGTH AND QUALITIES OF WOOD

Woodworkers must take a natural material and cut and shape it to best effect. To this end, the woodworker must appreciate that woodworking is an equal partnership, a coming together of tools, techniques and wood. It's no good trying to work wood with a dull tool, or to plane against the grain, or to run a chisel into end grain or in any way bully the wood into shape. The success of each and every procedure and technique hinges on the woodworker's understanding of how the inherent natural properties of the wood – its hardness, toughness, elasticity, durability and so on – can be used to best effect.

LEFT: Coarse-grained Honduras mahogany – not good for bending.

Hardness

Though hardwood comes from broad-leafed, deciduous trees, and softwood from evergreens, hardwood isn't necessarily harder or more difficult to work than softwood. When we describe a wood as being hard, we generally mean that the wood isn't easily dented or bruised on the end grain or face. So, for example, when a table design suggests that you build the surface from a wood that is hard, it means that you need to search out a wood that will resist surface impact. It could be a hard-surfaced softwood.

LEFT: End-grain pine with clearly defined annular rings – good for strength.

ABOVE: Quartersawn oak with characteristic medullary ray figure – strong and decorative.

Toughness

A tough wood is one that is difficult to split, a wood that has a lot of bending strength in relationship to its length. So, for example, English longbows were traditionally made from yew, golf club shafts from hickory and axe handles from ash – all tough wood types that are wonderfully resistant to crushing and splitting.

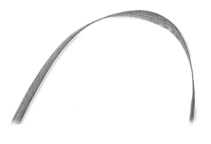

ABOVE: Some woods are specifically chosen for their bending qualities.

Bending

Bending and toughness are in many ways similar. But while some tough woods will happily resist a long, slow bend, they might well fail under what is termed a "shear impact". This being so, you must determine whether the item that you are building is going to be put under bending stress – as in a ladder – or is it going to support a heavy weight, such as a house beam.

ABOVE: A straight-grained wood will readily split along the grain.

Splitting

Sometimes called cleavage, the splitting qualities of a piece of wood are of paramount importance. You need to know when you are cutting a joint, or designing a piece that has an area of short grain, just how much strength there is between the bundles of fibres. For example, a straight-grained softwood like pine will easily split down the length of the grain, whereas a piece of maple will resist splitting.

Durability

The qualities that make a wood last come under the heading of durability. For example, elm survives under water; larch building pilings have survived for centuries; and cedar shingles seem to last forever. It's almost as if certain wood types

ABOVE: Boxwood is extremely close, even and dense in its grain – good for complex forms that show a lot of short grain.

enjoy being repeatedly wet, dried and baked in the sun. Some woods will last for hundreds of years underground or under water, but have a short life when exposed to wind and weather.

Resistance

The total strength of a piece of wood when put under a load is termed the resistance. To a great extent resistance brings together all the other qualities, including hardness, toughness, bending and durability. The question you should ask yourself every time you select a piece of wood is, "is it fit for its task?" The most reliable method of choosing wood for your window frame, or roof struts, is to see what was used in the past.

GOOD FINISH

If you ask a hundred woodworkers to define the term "good finish", you will get a hundred different definitions. And then if you ask the furniture-buying public to define "good finish", you will likely get even more definitions. Some may have to do with such notions and terms as smoothness, gloss and French polish perfection. It doesn't help too much either to look to the past for guidance, because whims and fashions then and now tend to be so contrary. For example, if you look at early American Windsor chairs, you will see that the chairmakers were quite happy to produce chairs that were less than symmetrical and surface textures that showed the marks left by the tools. On the other hand, if you look at late-nineteenth century furniture, you will see the woodworkers were seeking to achieve mechanically smooth finishes and/or finishes that fooled the eye into believing that, for example, a common softwood was an exotic hardwood.

Some authorities claim that the evolution of woodworking finishes necessarily reflects the shift from handtool techniques to mechanized techniques, with surfaces getting progressively smoother and more defined. But now we have come around to a curious state of affairs: while it is possible to achieve surfaces that are machined to absolute perfection, nevertheless there is a shift towards finishes that are rough sawn, gouge marked, wire brushed or otherwise heavily textured. Whereas gouge marks once said, "country made and provincial", the same gouge marks now say, "unique, handmade and special". This is not to say that you should in any way contrive to apply gouge marks or the like, but rather that you should start out on the premise that "form follows function". If, for example, a surface needs to be smooth – say for reasons of hygiene or for comfort – then fine. However, it's equally valid that surfaces be rippled, rough, matt, smooth or even stained with rust depending on the piece. All this adds up to the fact that you need to be aware of the possibilities for alternative surface textures. The following brief listing will point the way.

ABOVE: Rough sawn pine.

Rough Sawn

Rough sawn describes the wood as it leaves the lumberyard, meaning it is sawn to size, but hasn't yet been planed. Many woodworkers like to leave the saw marks to suggest a piece has either spent its life outdoors or at least that it might be used out of doors. Then again, some wood, like oak, gives the illusion that it is stronger and more rugged when it is left in the rough sawn state.

Planed

The act of planing cuts across the wood fibres, with the effect that the light is reflected off the surface of the wood and the character of the grain is highly visible. The more time spent planing, then the smoother the wood and so consequently the more radiant the grain. If you take this a step farther and start working the wood with a scraper plane, then the greater the depth and luminescence of the grain.

Wire Brushed

Wire brushing is the act of using a steel-bristled brush to distress the surface of the wood. Worked in the direction of the grain, the steel bristles cut and degrade the soft part of the grain, so the wood looks as if it has been ravaged by the elements. Take a piece of strong-grained wood like a piece of oak or pitch pine, give it a wire brushing, and it immediately looks as if it is a piece of driftwood or a piece of desert wood.

ABOVE: Gouge textured oak.

Gouge Textured

A sharp gouge creates a characteristic finish. If you have a good, long, close-up look at a piece of Northwest Coast carving as worked by the Native Americans or perhaps an early colonial chest, you will see a story in the tool marks. Not only do the gouge marks tell you how the various dips and hollows were achieved, but better yet, the pattern and rhythm of the tool marks give the surface a dynamic texture that is uniquely beautiful.

ABOVE: Wax polished.

Wax Polished

The soft and subtle deep sheen surfaces that we admire on antique furniture are often the result of a hundred or so years of wax polishing and burnishing. Natural beeswax is applied and the wood is rubbed with a brush and cloth.

Measuring and Marking

All woodworking starts with measurements. From the very outset of a project, you will need to use measuring and marking techniques, not only for preparing the materials and establishing dimensions, but also for laying out cutting lines and for testing that faces and edges are true. Once the wood has arrived, then comes the critical stage of using a whole range of tools and techniques for transferring the measurements from the working drawings to the wood. The fact that accuracy is crucial for good woodworking is very neatly summed up by the traditional adage, "Measure twice and cut once".

MEASURING RULES

Brass joints — Brass hinges

Metric and Imperial graduations

Brass tips

LEFT: Traditional four-fold boxwood and brass rule.

he traditional 61 cm (2-ft), four-fold boxwood and brass rule has long been considered the best all-round tool for measuring in woodwork. Of course, there are alternatives – folding extension rules, two-fold rules, tape measures, and many more besides. But nevertheless the four-fold rule is still the most economical, the

LEFT: The traditional boxwood rule is still a top quality tool. Place rule on edge for accurate markings.

easiest-to-use and the most versatile measuring tool for woodworking.

A good traditional method of using a rule to divide a board into a number of equal widths is as follows. Suppose a board is 15.25 cm (6-in) wide, and you want to divide it into seven equal widths. Set the rule across the board at an angle – so that 0 and 17.8 cm (7-in) are aligned with opposite edges of the board. Draw a line across the board and mark it off at 2.5 cm (1-in) intervals. Now use a marking gauge or a

long straight-edge to run parallel lines down the length of the board so that they intersect with the step-offs. Then the board will be divided into seven equal widths. If you use this technique, it doesn't matter if the board is an indeterminate width of anything less than 15.25 cm (6-in); the board will still be divided into seven equal parts.

LEFT: Make sure that the 0 and 17.8 cm (7–in) marks are perfectly aligned with the edges of the board.

RULES

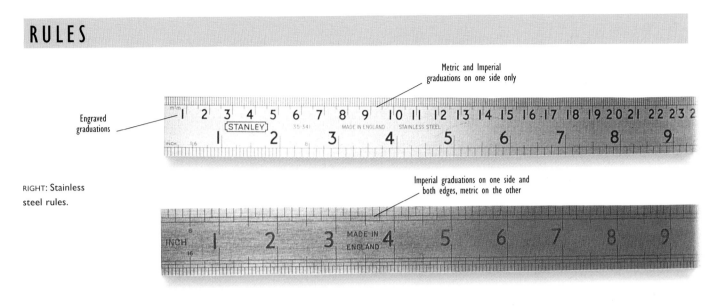

Metric and Imperial graduations on one side only

Engraved graduations

RIGHT: Stainless steel rules.

Imperial graduations on one side and both edges, metric on the other

STICKS

One of the easiest and most traditional ways of transferring a measurement from the working drawing to the wood, or from one piece of wood to another, is to use a measuring stick, sometimes called a story pole. Say that you want to make a copy of an existing item such as a chair rung. All

you need do, is set a stick alongside the rung, make a notch with a knife, and from then on in, all the other lengths can be marked off from the stick directly. And of course, if at the end of the project you label the stick with all the details and hang it on the wall with a loop of string, then next

time around, you can relate to the stick without the need for a rule or the rung. If the sticks are well labelled, then this system will save you a good deal of time and effort. In many ways this method of measuring is more accurate than working with a couple of rules that might differ slightly.

TAPES

One of the most commonly used measuring tools is the flexible tape – known usually as simply a "tape" or a "tape measure". In use, the end of the tape is hooked on the edge of the workpiece and then the hand-size body of the tape is drawn out in such a way that the sprung ribbon is pulled straight and stays rigid. Tapes like this are ideal for measuring surfaces that are curved – such as turned bowls or curved profiles. Unlike a wooden rule, the flexible tape can be wrapped around the object being measured.

BELOW: Power lock measuring tape. The tape measure is an indispensable tool.

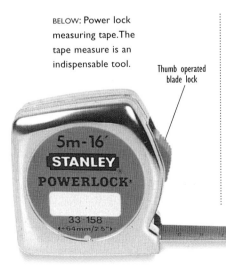

Thumb operated blade lock

True zero end hook

MARKING KNIVES

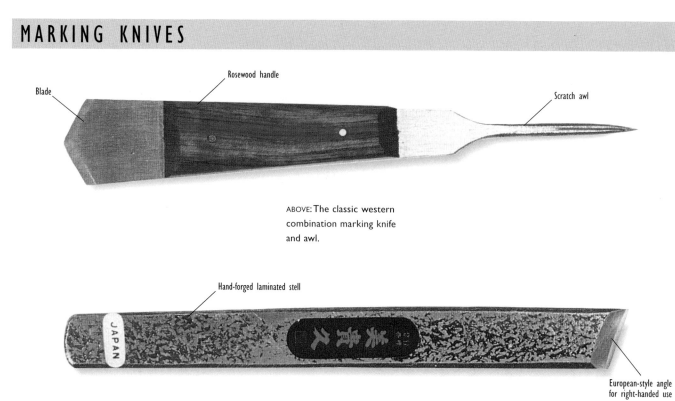

Blade

Rosewood handle

Scratch awl

ABOVE: The classic western combination marking knife and awl.

Hand-forged laminated stell

European-style angle for right-handed use

ABOVE: The Japanese marking knife.

The line of cut – meaning the line that will eventually need to be cut with a saw or chisel – should be marked out with a knife. Certainly the initial layout can be done with a hard-point pencil. But when the pencil lines are in place, and you have identified the cutting line, then the pencil lines will need to be reworked with the knife. If you use the knife the scored line will not only more positively establish the position of the line of cut, but better yet, the severed fibres of the wood will provide a starting point for the saw or chisel, reducing the potential for chipping.

LEFT: Use the fingers of the left hand to pull the bevel hard up against the workpiece.

Although marking knives come in all shapes and sizes, the very best type has a bevel on one side only, so that the flat face of the blade can be run hard up against the straight edge.

Many woodworkers worldwide are now coming around to the idea that the Japanese marking knife is the best tool for the job. These knives – designed for left-, right- or double-handed use – are razor sharp with a hollow-ground bevel. In use, the square or metal straight edge is positioned on the line to be marked, the flat side of the marking knife is held hard against the edge, and then the line is struck – or you might say scored – by the knife drawn towards you in a single, uninterrupted stroke.

If you relate more to the Western tradition, and if you like the idea of a dual purpose tool, then you might consider a combined marking knife and awl. With a double-bevel blade at one end and a taper awl spike at the other, this is a great tool for a whole range of marking, scribing, scratching and spiking tasks.

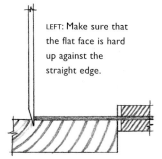

LEFT: Make sure that the flat face is hard up against the straight edge.

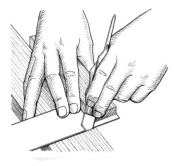

ABOVE: The traditional marking knife cum awl is still an indispensable tool. It is good for both left- and right-handed use.

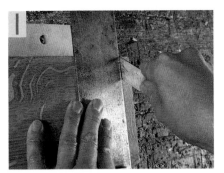

1 Set the square down on the workpiece so that the metal straight edge is positioned on the drawn line, then position the knife so that the flat face is hard up against the straight edge, and finally draw the knife towards you in a single stroke.

2 Butt the workpiece against the bench hook, then use the previously scored line to align the saw blade.

SCRIBES AND AWLS

Known variously as marking awls, striking awls, scratch awls or simply as awls, these are pointed tools that are used to scratch lines and spike holes. The most basic form – called a scratch awl – has a 12.7 cm (5-in), needle-like spike and a ball-shaped handle. In use, the handle is cupped in the palm of the hand with the index finger extended along the spike. Then the tool is either drawn to make a line or swiveled on the spot to make a hole. A slight variation is a chisel-pointed version called a bradawl, which is used for spiking holes in heavily grained hardwood.

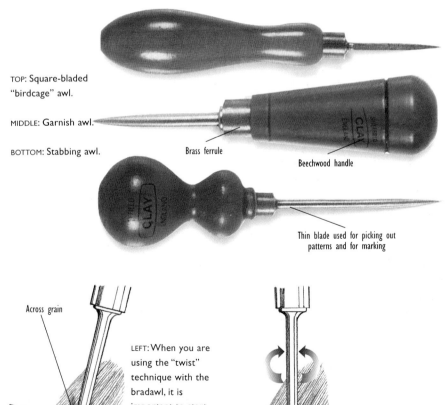

TOP: Square-bladed "birdcage" awl.

MIDDLE: Garnish awl.

BOTTOM: Stabbing awl.

Brass ferrule

Beechwood handle

Thin blade used for picking out patterns and for marking

LEFT: The scratch awl is the perfect tool to spike pilot holes in softwood to start nails and screws.

Across grain

LEFT: When you are using the "twist" technique with the bradawl, it is important to start the twist with the chisel point set across the run of the grain.

LEFT: Having initiated the cut across the grain, twist to make the mark.

SQUARES

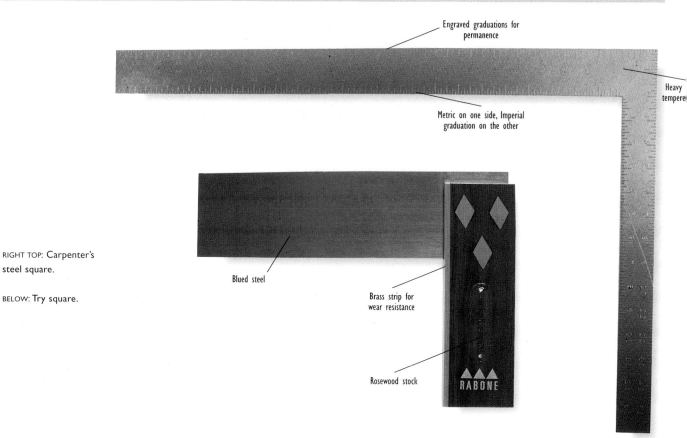

Engraved graduations for
permanence

Metric on one side, Imperial
graduation on the other

Heavy
tempere

Blued steel

Brass strip for
wear resistance

Rosewood stock

RABONE

RIGHT TOP: Carpenter's
steel square.

BELOW: Try square.

Carpenter's Steel Square

The woodworker is forever needing to use one or other of a whole range of squares to variously test that lines, edges and faces are at right angles to each other. The simplest square, known as a carpenter's square, is simply a single piece of "L" shaped steel that is marked out with various measurements and tables. The carpenter's square is designed primarily to be used for large work – table tops, cupboard frames and doors. The short arm is known as the "tongue", while the long arm is known as the "blade". Being made from a single piece of steel, a square of this character is just about as strong, precise and foolproof as a square can get. Better yet, the large size of the square – the tongue is 40.65 cm (16-in) long and the blade is 60.95cm (24-in) long – ensures a high degree of accuracy. If you are new to woodwork, and if you are looking to get yourself a square, and if you

have in mind to build big, then remember that the longer the arms of the square, the longer the contact with the workpiece, and so consequently the greater the accuracy.

Try Square

The familiar try square with its steel blade and rosewood handle – the handle is called a "stock" – all fitted and fixed with fancy brass inlay and rivets, is designed primarily for bench work. If you want to mark lines that run at right angles to edges and faces,

ABOVE: Butt the long arm hard
up against the side of the wood.

then this is the tool for the job. To use the try square, first plane and mark the true face and edge of the wood. Then press the try square's stock hard up against the true face, striking lines off against the steel blade. The superior try square has an "L" shaped blade, one arm of which is encased in the wood. Lesser models have a strip of metal that is top-mounted to the wood. You can appreciate that if the poor grade square is dropped, then the chances are that the blade will be knocked askew.

ABOVE: Hold the square so that the wooden
handle – sometimes known as a "stock" –
is hard up against the workpiece.

COMBINATION SQUARE

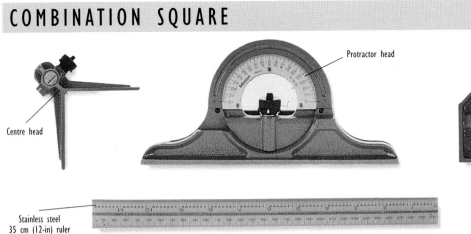

Centre head

Protractor head

Square head incorporating a spirit level and scriber

ABOVE: The "square" head is used to mark right angles and mitres.

Stainless steel 35 cm (12-in) ruler

The all-metal combination square with its rule and three measuring heads is a beautiful three-in-one tool. It's great for all manner of marking and layout tasks. The "centre head" allows you to establish the centre point of round sections such as dowels and turnings. The "protractor head" can be used for marking off all the angles through to 180 degrees. The "square head" with its spirit level can be used to mark right angles and 45-degree mitres. The "blade" can be used as a depth gauge and to check the alignment of such details as mortises and shoulders. And of course, if you remove all the heads, then you have a metal straightedge. In use, you simply select the head, loosen the thumbscrew, slide the head in place along the rule, retighten the screw and get on with the task at hand.

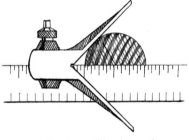

ABOVE: The "centre" head is used to establish the centre point and the diameter line of round sections.

T-BEVEL

The T-bevel or bevel gauge is another tool used for marking and laying out angles. The tool comes either with the blade pivoted to the middle of the wooden stock, or with the blade slotted so that it slides along the pivot. To draw an angle, the wing nut or screw is loosened, the blade is set to the required angle against a protractor, the nut is retightened and then the angle can be transferred to the workpiece. Remember that for any single setting, you always have the two angles that go to make up 180 degrees. To verify an angle from an existing workpiece, or to read off an angle from a drawing, the nut is loosened, the blade and the wooden stock are pushed hard up against the workpiece in or over the angle, the nut is retightened and a protractor is used to check the resulting angle.

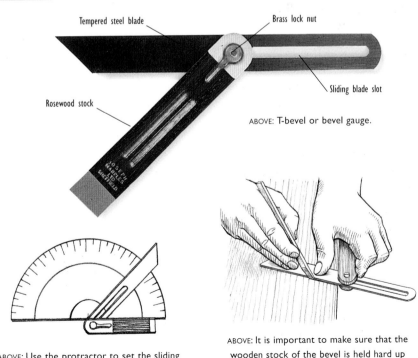

Tempered steel blade

Brass lock nut

Rosewood stock

Sliding blade slot

ABOVE: T-bevel or bevel gauge.

ABOVE: Use the protractor to set the sliding bevel blade to the desired angle.

ABOVE: It is important to make sure that the wooden stock of the bevel is held hard up against the edge of the workpiece.

GAUGES

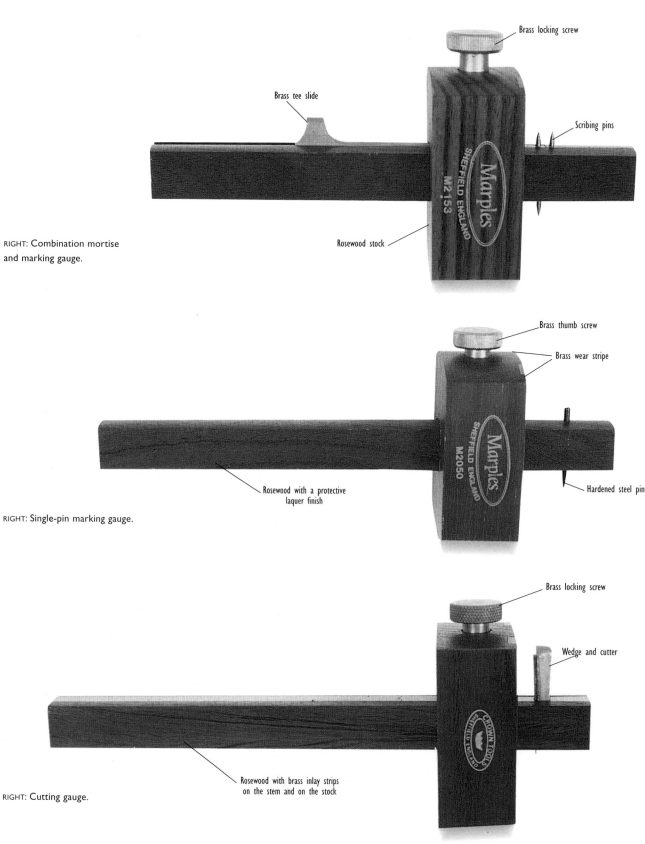

Brass locking screw

Brass tee slide

Scribing pins

Rosewood stock

RIGHT: Combination mortise
and marking gauge.

Brass thumb screw

Brass wear stripe

Rosewood with a protective
laquer finish

Hardened steel pin

RIGHT: Single-pin marking gauge.

Brass locking screw

Wedge and cutter

Rosewood with brass inlay strips
on the stem and on the stock

RIGHT: Cutting gauge.

Setting the Single-pin Marking Gauge

There are two primary ways of setting a marking gauge: You can either set the distance by taking a direct reading from the edge of a rule, or better still, you can make a mark on scrapwood, and then set the gauge to the mark. Let's say then that you want to go for the latter technique, and you want to run a line 2.55 cm (1-in) in from the edge of the wood. The procedure is simple: first use a square ruler and pencil to make a mark 2.55 cm (1-in) in from the edge of the wood. Then loosen the thumbscrew, spike the pin on the mark, slide the fence hard up against the edge of the wood, tighten the screw, and finally have a trial run on a piece of scrap to test the setting.

Setting and Using the Mortise Gauge

The mortise gauge has two pins – one fixed and the other movable. To use the tool, set the distance between the two pins to the width of your chisel. Adjust the fence so that the pins are centred on the middle of the workpiece. When you are happy with the adjustment, butt the mortise fence hard up against the face side of the wood, and then draw the gauge away from you with an even dragging stroke. It's important that the pin is dragged rather than pushed.

Using the Cutting Gauge

Let's say you want to cut a 2.55 cm (1-in)-wide strip from a 32 mm (¹/₈-in)-thick piece of stock or from a piece of veneer. Having first of all honed the cutter to a razor sharp edge, refit it in the stem and set the fence so that it is 2.55 cm (1-in) away from the cutter. This done, support the veneer so that the true edge is flush with the cutting board, butt the fence hard up against the board, and then drag it away from you – in much the same way as when using the marking gauge. Repeat the procedure until the strip is free.

ABOVE: Spike the pin on the mark, slide the fence against the edge and tighten the screw.

ABOVE: Adjust the two pins directly from the chisel.

ABOVE: Repeatedly run the gauge along the edge until the veneer is cut through.

DIVIDERS

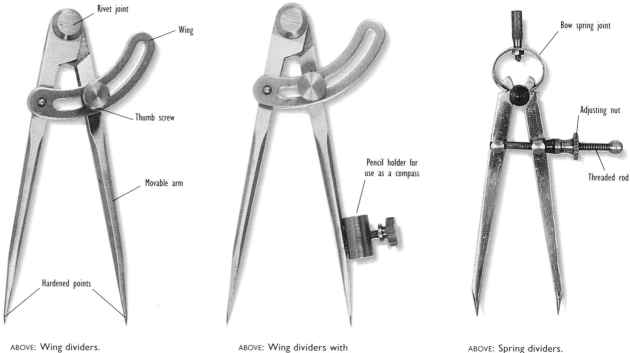

ABOVE: Wing dividers.

ABOVE: Wing dividers with pencil holder.

ABOVE: Spring dividers.

Laying out a Hexagon

Dividers are used primarily for reading measurements off a rule, for transferring measurements and for scribing out circles and arcs. If you are thinking of getting a pair of dividers, get the type that have a screw-thread adjustment and a locking nut.

1 Set the legs or points of the dividers to the desired radius measurement.

2 Spike the dividers down on the workpiece and scribe out the circle.

3 Spike the dividers down on the scribed circle, then step the radius off around the circumference to make six equal intersections.

4 Use a straight edge to link up adjoining step-offs to result in the hexagon.

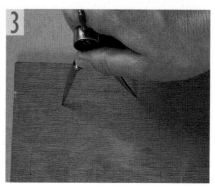

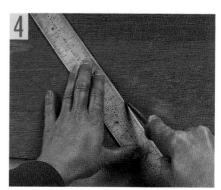

CALLIPERS

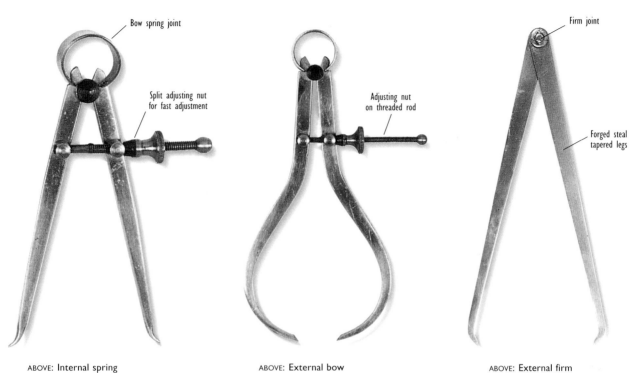

Bow spring joint

Split adjusting nut
for fast adjustment

Adjusting nut
on threaded rod

Firm joint

Forged steal
tapered legs

ABOVE: Internal spring
bow callipers.

ABOVE: External bow
spring callipers.

ABOVE: External firm
joint callipers.

Precision callipers are needed for reliable laying out and for accurate measuring. There are three main types: "outside" callipers, which are used to measure the diameter of solid objects; the "inside" callipers that are used to measure the diameters inside holes and the "double-sided" callipers that are used by woodturners to pinch the wall thickness of a bowl and to transfer measurements from one tip to the other.

LEFT: To measure the outside diameter, hook the arms of the callipers around the workpiece so the workpiece is cradled, then open the arms until the workpiece just slips free.

TIPS BOX

If you want a trammel just for one job, then you can get by with an easy-to-make item. All you need is a length of wood with a nail tapped through one end, holes drilled at 1.27 cm (¹/₂-in) intervals along the wood, and a pencil or large nail to fit the holes.

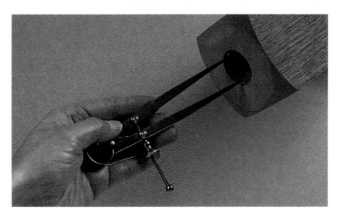

LEFT: To measure the inside diameter, slide the feet into the hole, undo the screw until the little feet are a snug fit then draw them out of the hole.

TRAMMEL POINTS

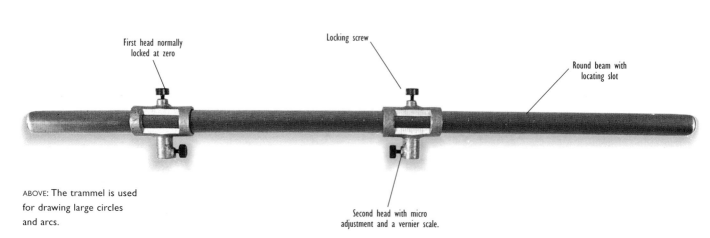

First head normally locked at zero

Locking screw

Round beam with locating slot

Second head with micro adjustment and a vernier scale.

ABOVE: The trammel is used for drawing large circles and arcs.

Known also as a beam compass, the trammel is the perfect traditional tool for drawing large circles and arcs, and for creating circle-based motifs. Trammel points also help with equilateral triangles, hexagons, six-point stars, gothic tracery and all manner of geometrical forms. The trammel technique is beautifully simple; all you need is the trammel, a straight edge and a pencil.

Drawing a Folk Art Circle-Hex Star

It's easy to scribe a large circle-hex star, as in the Pennsylvania American folk art tradition, to fit into a 60.95 cm (2-ft)-diameter circle – perhaps for a motif on a square table top. First use a pencil and straightedge to draw crossed diagonals to establish the centre of the table. Then set the trammel points to a radius of 30.5 cm (12-in) and scribe the 60.95 cm (2-ft)-diameter circle. Now spike one point on the circumference and travel around striking off arcs. Lastly, take the pencil and straightedge – or you might use a knife if the surface is to be veneered – and link up every other intersection so that you have a six-point star

Drawing a Hexagon

Let's say you want to draw a hexagon that fits in a 60.95 cm (2-ft)-diameter circle, perhaps for a table top. First fix the trammel points – the steel point and the pencil – to a radius of 30.5 cm (12-in). Then scribe the circle. Next, with the points still fixed to the same radius, spike the steel point on the circumference of the circle and travel around striking off arcs. You should finish up with six step-offs. Lastly, use a pencil and straightedge to link neighbouring intersections.

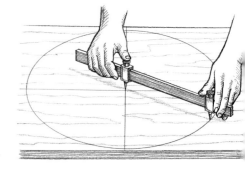

ABOVE: Spike one trammel point down on the centre and swing the other point to scribe the circle.

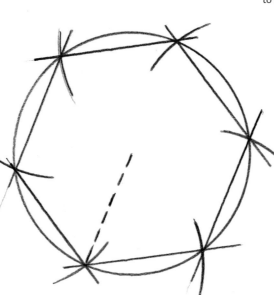

LEFT: Link up neighbouring intersections with straight lines to produce a hexagon.

JIGS

A jig is a simple device designed to hold and position a component while it is being worked. A jig also can be a device used to facilitate a procedure that needs to be repeated. The whole idea of a jig is that it speeds up work by allowing you to swiftly grip and position the workpiece while you perform a repetitious task.

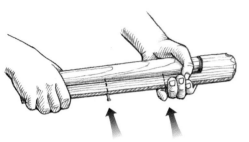

ABOVE: Chair leg jig. Set the leg in the jig, press them together so that the nail points mark the position of the stretcher holes.

Chair Leg Jig

The chair leg jig – as used traditionally by the English bodgers – is simply an "L"-shaped stick with a foot on one end and a couple of nails banged through the upright. To use the jig, the bodger took a chair leg – he made a leg unit every four or five minutes – located it on the foot of the jig and then squeezed the leg and the jig together so that the nail points marked the precise position of the stretcher holes. If you are faced with the task of marking off a series of repeat measurements – such as fence posts, or component parts for a cupboard, or turned spindles, or toy parts – then a jig like this is a great easy-to-make time saver.

Cross Jig

The cross jig – made up from two pieces of wood that are crossed one over the other and fixed with screws – is used to run a line around the edge of the workpiece in much the same way as a marking gauge. In use, the jig is pressed hard up against an edge, the pencil is located in a hole or in a notch,

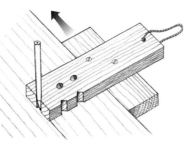

ABOVE: Cross jig: Slide the jig hard up against the workpiece so that the pencil marks a line that is parallel to the edge.

and then the whole works is moved along so that the pencil makes a mark. A jig of this type is a good, easy-to-make tool for such tasks as marking the width of a chamfer, marking a rebate or marking the position of an inlay.

Mitre Jig

The 45 degree-mitred cut is just about the most common cut that you are likely to make, so it follows that you need to get yourself a mitre box jig. The jig is simply a "U"-shaped channel with one or more slots running across the channel at 45 degrees. In use, the workpiece is positioned and held in the channel, a saw is run through the guide slot and the cut is made. This jig is easy to use and perfect for picture frames, mitred joints, beading mitres and a whole host of other mitring tasks.

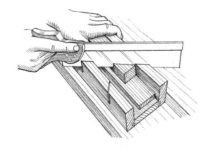

ABOVE: Miter jig. The strip of waste wood under the workpiece saves the jig from saw damage.

Drilling Jig

The drilling jig is designed to position and hold a component part for drilling a hole. The jig is clamped to the drill press table, the workpiece is pushed up against the stop and clamped or held in position, and then the hole is drilled. The joy of this type of jig is the fact that it can be made from scrap and be up and running in moments. If you want the hole to run through the component part at an angle greater or smaller then 90 degrees – let's say for the splayed legs of a Windsor chair – all you do is cut an angled wedge to fix between the jig and the worktable.

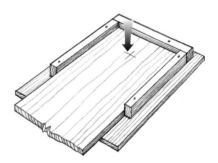

ABOVE: Batch run drilling jig – used for drilling repeat holes in a number of identical boards.

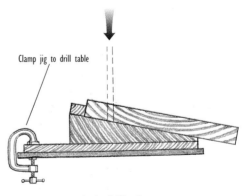

Clamp jig to drill table

ABOVE: Angle-drilling jig – the jig allows you to drill repeat holes at the same angle.

Clamping

Clamping techniques are used at nearly every stage of woodworking. Don't get confused by the names – bench vice, screw clamps, G- or C-clamps, hold-downs, hold-fasts, sash clamps, handscrews, pipe clamps, rope-and-wedge clamps, vice-clamps – they are all devices for variously holding the wood secure. The more clamps you have, the greater your control and the more work options you have.

THE VICE

Sawing in a Vice

When sawing in the vice you can minimize vibration and chatter by keeping the workpiece as low as possible. But unfortunately what sometimes happens is that the workpiece is positioned to one side of the screw, potentially putting the mechanism under damaging strain. In this situation, it's good practice to equalize the strain and maintain balance by setting a piece of scrap to the other side of the screw. Some woodworkers keep a selection of off-cuts specifically for this purpose.

Planing End Grain in a Vice

Although the vice is great for holding short end-grain work, especially when using a block plane, care has to be taken that the plane doesn't split off fibres at the end of its run. The best procedure is to clamp a sacrificial waster in the vice alongside the workpiece and flush with the top of the workpiece. That way the plane skims first across the workpiece and then across the waste. What happens, of course, is that the waste is damaged rather than the workpiece.

Cutting Joinery in a Vice

When using a heavy mallet and chisel to cut a deep mortise, it is handy to grip the workpiece in the top of the vice. Often the force of the blows knocks the workpiece askew. The power behind the mallet blow is then depleted, the workpiece is damaged, and time and energy are wasted. To remedy the situation, position one or more blocks of waste between the workpiece and the vice bars to provide solid underside support without inhibiting clamping action.

ABOVE: The wood set to the left of the vice screw saves the mechanism from damage.

ABOVE: This set-up ensures that the damage occurs on the waster, rather than the workpiece.

ABOVE: The block of waste under the workpiece takes the brunt of the blows.

Paring in a Vice

When you use a bevel-edge chisel to pare the waste from a groove that runs across the grain, it's often a good idea to use a bench hook in the vice to support the work. Set the hook in the vice, then run parallel saw cuts across the workpiece to establish the width and depth of the groove. Next, butt the workpiece hard up against the stop, and hold the chisel parallel with the bottom of the groove. Finally, either push or use mallet taps to clear the waste. Work from both sides toward the middle to avoid exit damage.

ABOVE: The bench hook stop prevents tool-exit damage.

Using a Drawknife in a Vice

If you want to use a drawknife to swiftly cut a chair leg or some other piece to a round section, then the problem is how to hold the workpiece at the correct angle. The answer is beautifully simple. All you do is first clamp a strip of wood across the bench so that it bridges the top of the vice. Then set the workpiece in the jaws, adjusting the workpiece so that it's held securely at the correct angle and supported by the bridge piece. Once you have worked one end with the knife, then just turn the wood around and rerun the procedure for the other end.

ABOVE: Work with a series of little-by-little strokes.

Drilling in a Vice

One of the problems when using the brace and bit is how to hold and support the workpiece so that you can put the full weight of your body behind the brace. One good way is to back the workpiece with a substantial piece of waste and then set the assembly in the vice so that the hole to be drilled is a little above the height of your waist. This set-up is a winner on several counts: The wood is well supported, the backing piece prevents tear-out damage when the bit exits and, best of all, you can achieve optimum control and pressure by supporting the brace pad on your abdomen.

ABOVE: For maximum efficiency, the waste piece needs to run down to the floor.

BENCH STOPS AND DOGS

Bench stops and dogs are variously wood or metal rods, pillars and blocks that stand up proud from the surface of the bench and against which the workpiece is butted, gripped or otherwise held. Although there are many types – some with springs, others with swivel pads and screws – they all function more or less in the same way. In use, the workpiece – usually a panel or board – is set flat-side-down on the bench and then butted hard up against the stop or dogs.

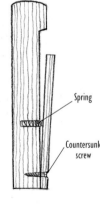

LEFT: Using a bench stop.

Vice Dog

A vice dog is specific to certain types of vices. To use the dog, the vice is first opened up so that it is well clear of the edge of the bench, and the dog is raised. The workpiece is set flat-side-down so that it is butted against the bench stops and projecting over the edge of the bench. Then the vice is closed so that the workpiece is clamped between the bench stop and the vice dog. The vice dog is great for holding wood for planing or joinery.

Stop-and-Wedge

A stop-and-wedge is an easy-to-make system for securing a workpiece. All you need is a pattern of square holes in the worktop, a number of wooden dogs to fit, and a good selection of different size wedges. The technique is wonderfully direct. All you do is butt the workpiece against a couple of stops, set two stops as near as you can to the other side of the workpiece, and then bang wedges in between the stops and the workpiece. The beauty of this arrangement is that it can be swiftly adjusted to suit almost any size workpiece.

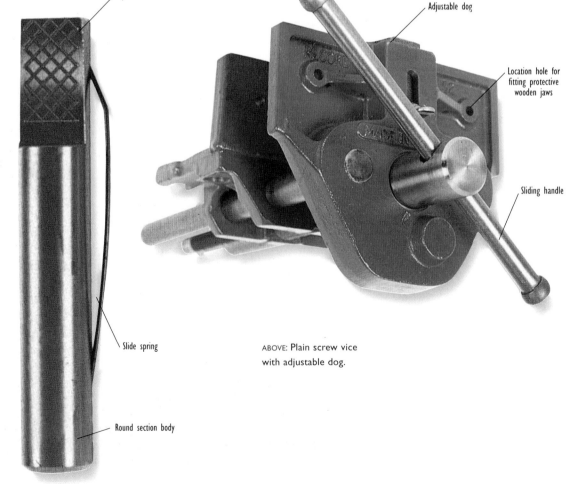

ABOVE: Quick-release bench stop made of wood.

RIGHT: Bench dog designed to fit in a drill hole.

ABOVE: Plain screw vice with adjustable dog.

Batten and Wedge

Small flat work can be secured quickly and easily with a traditional system known either as batten and wedge or bar and folding wedge. First, a batten is screwed to the bench surface, then the workpiece is butted hard up against the batten. Next, another batten is screwed onto the bench 2.55 cm (1-in) or so at the other side of the workpiece. This done, two pairs of wedges called folding wedges are set point to point, positioned between the workpiece and the batten, and tapped towards each other until the whole arrangement is secure. This system is a winner on many counts: the battens can be fitted in a matter of moments; there is minimum damage to the bench – no need to cut holes; the wedges can be made quickly and reused; the arrangement can be easily modified for just about any size of workpiece; and best of all, the whole works can be made from scrap.

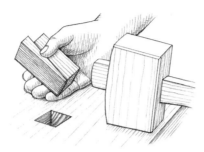

ABOVE: Home-made bench stop – two wedge type.

1 Drill and screw the first batten to the bench.

2 Drill and screw the second batten to the bench so that the workpiece fits loosely between the battens.

3 Set the workpiece in place between the two battens and slide the pair of folding wedges in place.

4 Tap the wedges toward each other until the whole arrangement is tightly clamped.

WOODEN HANDSCREW

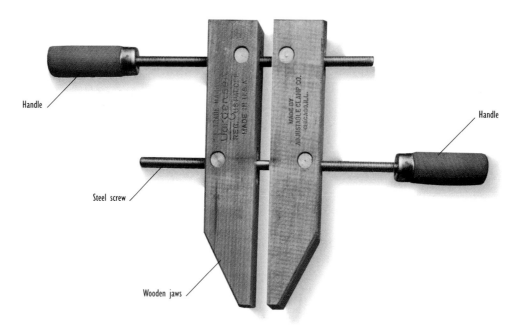

ABOVE: A modern handscrew – with
hard maple jaws and a deep throat.

The classic wooden handscrew is the
perfect tool for gluing and assembly.
The long-nosed wooden jaws distribute
the pressure evenly without twist-
crushing, and the wood-to-wood contact
cuts out the risk of iron-on-metal staining.
In use, the jaws are quickly operated by
holding both handles and pedalling one
about the other – as if turning the pedals
of a bicycle with your hands. Once the
primary tightening has been managed
with the inner screw, then the final turn-
to-clinch clamping is done with the
outer screw.

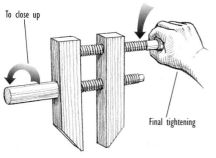

ABOVE: Wooden handscrew – the two-handed
tightening sequence.

Clamping When Gluing

The unique action of the traditional
wooden handscrew results in the jaws
moving directly in and out. There is no
twisting force applied to the workpiece, as
with most other clamps. This particular
function makes the handscrew the ideal
clamp for holding glued wood that needs to
be carefully positioned.

Clamping at an Angle

Another feature of the handscrew is that
the jaws can be screwed in so they meet the
workpiece at an angle. For example, if you
need to grip a long pie-shaped piece, then
the jaws and the workpiece would come
together with all mating faces in full
contact. This unique function makes the
handscrew ideally suited for clamping
uneven and unparallel forms.

ABOVE: Clamping when gluing.

ABOVE: Clamping at an angle.

BENCH HOLDFAST

The bench holdfast – sometimes called a hold-down – is the perfect clamp for flat work. The workpiece is set flat-down on the bench, and the lever arm with its swivel shoe is placed on the work. Then the screw is given a couple of swift turns. The action of the screw decreases the angle between the main shaft and the arm to apply clamping force. The holdfast is relatively inexpensive, it can be fitted in moments, it can be raised to take any thickness of wood and, best of all, it can be positioned and repositioned in seconds.

To fit the holdfast, a hole must be bored right through the bench top. Then a ring-plate collar is screwed into position over the hole so that it is flush with the surface. Finally, the notched shaft is slid down through the collar. If you are a carver or cabinetmaker and you want optimum flexibility, you could have half a dozen or more holdfast holes scattered around the bench.

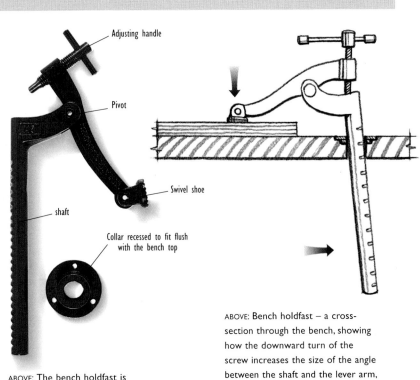

Adjusting handle

Pivot

Swivel shoe

shaft

Collar recessed to fit flush with the bench top

ABOVE: The bench holdfast is used primarily for flat work.

ABOVE: Bench holdfast – a cross-section through the bench, showing how the downward turn of the screw increases the size of the angle between the shaft and the lever arm, effectively securing the workpiece.

THE HAND VICE

Though the all-metal hand vice – also called a drill press vice or a machinist's vice – is by rights a metalworking tool, many woodworkers consider them a useful

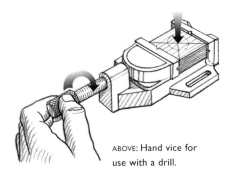

ABOVE: Hand vice for use with a drill.

addition to their woodshop. The hand vice has a heavy metal base plate, a pair of grooved and notched jaws that are set in a track and a handscrew. The workpiece is either set horizontally or vertically in the jaws, and then the screw is tightened.

The hand vice is an essential tool for drilling large-diameter holes on the bench drill press. If you want to drill holes larger than 1.2 cm ($^1/_2$-in) diameter, then securing the workpiece in the hand vice is the safest way to go, especially if the workpiece is small and difficult to hold. For example, if you wanted to bore a 5.1-cm (2-in)-diameter hole through a component that is not much bigger than the hole – say about 10.15-cm (4-in) across – then the hand vice is the tool for the job.

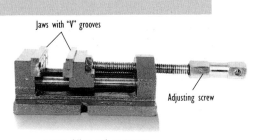

Jaws with "V" grooves

Adjusting screw

ABOVE: All-metal engineers hand vice.

TIPS BOX

WARNING – Never attempt to drill a large hole on the drill press without first securing the workpiece in a hand vice and then clamping the hand vice to the drill press table. Most vices are fitted with bolt slots for easy mounting and alignment.

C-CLAMPS

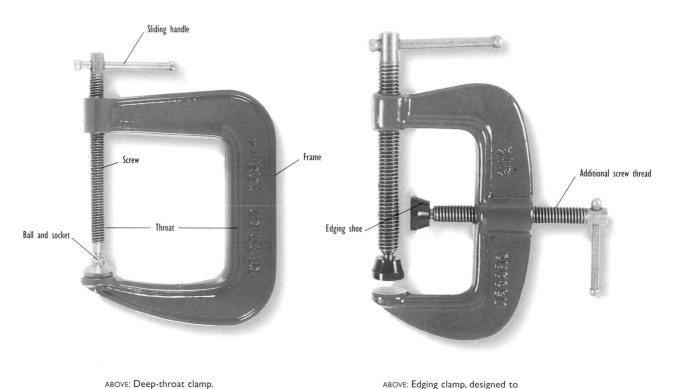

Sliding handle

Screw

Frame

Ball and socket

Throat

Additional screw thread

Edging shoe

ABOVE: Deep-throat clamp.

ABOVE: Edging clamp, designed to secure strips on edges.

Metal C-clamps are the primary clamp for woodworking. There are big ones with small throats, small ones with deep throats, ones with tommy or cross bars for tightening the screw, ones with butterfly wing nuts, and all manner of sizes, shapes and types in between. When buying clamps there are one or two pointers that you need to heed. The clamp must have a forged frame, and the ball-and-socket shoe fixture at the end of the screw must be centred on the anvil. Remember that, as most jobs need clamping at both ends, you usually need to buy clamps in pairs.

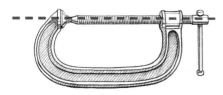

ABOVE: Clamp – it's vital that the screw and the ball-and socket fixture are centred on the anvil.

Good Clamping Practice

It is important that you use the correct size clamp for the job. If the workpiece isn't holding, then either you need to use additional clamps and/or you need a larger size. Never be tempted to use a wrench or bar to tighten the screw. Remember that clamps can exert many hundreds of pounds

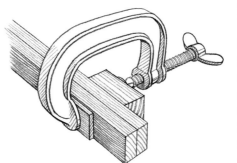

ABOVE: Always have a piece of waste wood between the clamp and the workpiece.

pressure – enough to crush some wood types – so it is always a good idea to set blocks of waste wood between the clamp heads and the workpiece. If the clamping procedure requires that you have to turn the screw more that about three-quarters in, then you either need to use a smaller clamp, or have more packing between the shoe and the workpiece.

Edge C-Clamps

Edge C-clamps are similar to conventional C-clamps in shape and structure, but edge clamps are designed specifically to hold strips in place on the edge of the workpiece. For example, to glue a strip to the edge of a table, the C-frame is first clamped to the table top, the glued strip is positioned on the edge, and then an additional screw is tightened up so that the strip is pushed against the edge.

STEEL BAR CLAMPS

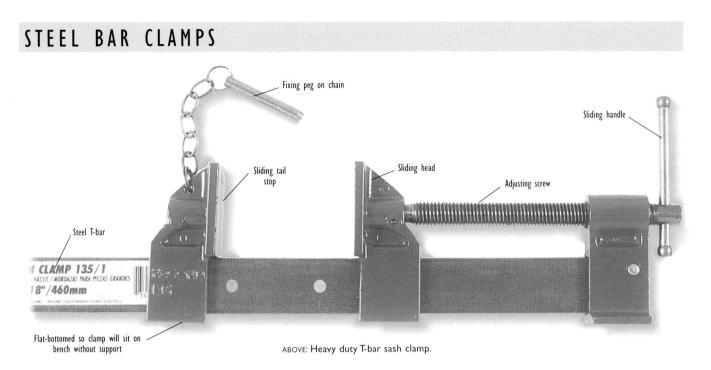

Fixing peg on chain

Sliding handle

Sliding tail stop

Sliding head

Adjusting screw

Steel T-bar

CLAMP 135/1
HÁSSIS / MORDAZAS PARA MEZAS GRANDES
18"/460mm

Flat-bottomed so clamp will sit on bench without support

ABOVE: **Heavy duty** T-bar sash clamp.

Although steel bar clamps come in all shapes and sizes, they are all similar in structure. There is usually a long round or rectangular section bar, a fixed screw head and clamp at one end of the bar, a fixed stop-pin at the other end and a sliding tail stop or jaw in between. In use, the head clamp is unscrewed, the workpiece is set in place, the tail stop slides up to the workpiece and then pressure is applied by tightening up the headscrew.

I Set a piece of waste between the tail stop and the workpiece.

2 First unscrew the clamp head to its full extent. Slide a piece of waste between it and the workpiece, then tighten up the screw.

3 Secure all three clamps, one on top and twop underneath, to prevent buckling. Make adjustments until the whole assembly is square and true.

Sawing

Before wood can be planed, laid out with the design, jointed, fretted and otherwise shaped, it first has to be sawn from the rough board. There are all manner of saws, each designed for a specific task. Because sawing is pivotal to all the other woodworking procedures, it is critical that you build up a good collection of quality handsaws and spend time perfecting the various sawing techniques.

RIPSAWING AND CROSSCUTTING

The ripsaw is designed specifically for cutting along the length of the grain. The teeth are filed at 90 degrees across the blade so that each tooth is square-cut, meaning without a bevel on the side face. In use, the teeth act just like a series of chisels, with each tooth cutting directly into the grain and removing the waste as shavings or strands of fibre in much the same way as a paring chisel. If you intend to cut parallel with the fibres of the wood – down a plank, or down a block – then a ripsaw is the tool for the job.

Crosscut

The crosscut saw is designed to cut across the grain. The teeth are filed at an angle of about 65 degrees across the blade. In use, the crosscut teeth first sever the fibres by scoring each side of the cut, and then remove the waste by reducing it to fine particles. Most woodworkers will require a selection of crosscut saws to handle different size jobs.

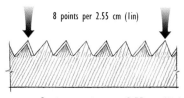

ABOVE: Sawing – points per 2.55 cm (1in)

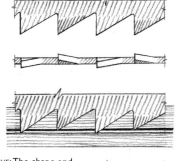

ABOVE: The shape and profile of the ripsaw blade results in a chisel-paring cut.

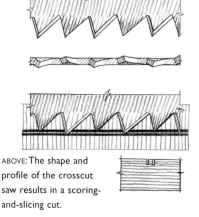

ABOVE: The shape and profile of the crosscut saw results in a scoring-and-slicing cut.

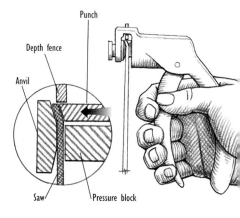

ABOVE: The saw set in action.

SHARPENING SAWS

Saw sharpening is always done in three sequential stages: jointing, fitting and setting.

1 Jointing ensures that the teeth are the same height. Sandwich the saw between two pieces of wood held in the vice, then use a flat file to cut all the teeth down to the same level. The jointing procedure usually takes no more than a few strokes of the file.

RIGHT:
Jointing the ripsaw.

2 Fitting makes sure that all teeth are at the correct angle. Use a triangular-section, 60-degree file to cut the leading edge of each tooth to the correct angle. The angle that the file is held in its approach to the saw blade varies according to the type of saw being sharpened. Ripsaw teeth are filed at an approach angle of 90 degrees, meaning the file is held at right angles to the saw blade. Crosscut teeth are filed at an approach angle of about 45 degrees. Alternate teeth are worked from one side of the blade, and then the whole procedure is rerun from the other side. With crosscut saws, the leading edge of each tooth is canted back by about 12 degrees.

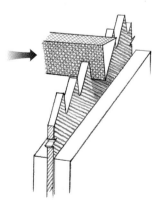

ABOVE: Fitting the ripsaw.

RIGHT: Saw-tooth setter – a foolproof tool for setting the teeth.

3 Setting adjusts the teeth for proper cutting clearance. Use a plier-like tool called a "saw set" to splay the teeth. The jaws of the set are opened, the tool is located on the tooth, and then the handles are clenched to bend the tooth over at an angle. The teeth need to be set alternately left and right down the length of the blade. The angle of set determines the width of the kerf and amount of cutting clearance. Use a generous set for cutting greenwood and a small set for cutting well-seasoned hardwood.

ABOVE: Setting the ripsaw.

TIPS BOX

Many woodworkers advocate a mix of hand saws and power saws. So for example, they might use a bandsaw to rough-out a piece, an electric scroll saw to cut out the primary form, and then they follow with the hand tools. This way of working is a good idea – even if you are a woodworking traditionalist – because the power tools allow you to spend more time on the quality-time tasks.

THE RIPSAW

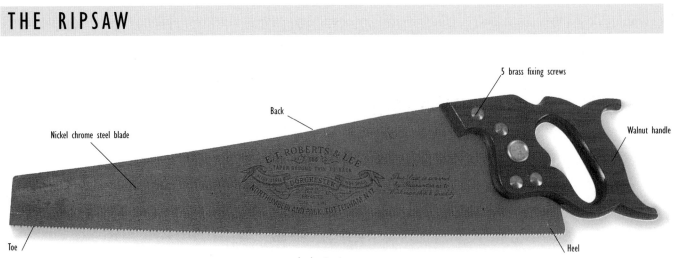

5 brass fixing screws

Back

Nickel chrome steel blade

Walnut handle

Toe

Heel

ABOVE: A classic ripsaw.

A ripsaw is designed to efficiently cut wood along its length. If you need to cut wood in the direction of the grain, then look for a ripsaw that has the following features: teeth that are filed at right angles across the saw blade, a well-detailed good-to-hold wooden handle, a good number of shoulder bolts that fix the handle to the blade, and a ground, tapered blade that is straight and flexible. Although the size of the saw is a matter of personal choice, here's a good general guide: about 66 cm (26 in) long with 5 tooth points to 2.55 cm (1 in) for cabinet work and 4 points to 2.55 cm (1 in) for carpentry – when you might expect the wood to be damp.

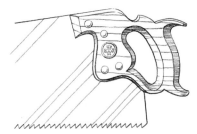

ABOVE: A better quality saw is characterized by the good number of bolts securing the handle to the blade.

Stance

It is important when using the ripsaw to support the workpiece at a comfortable height. In most instances, you need to have the board supported on a pair of saw-horses, at a height that prevents the toe of the blade from touching the ground. Set the work at an angle and height that lets you look directly down on the line to be cut while at the same time enabling you to get your shoulder behind the thrust.

ABOVE: Using the ripsaw –
front view of correct
stance.

ABOVE: Using the ripsaw –
side view of correct stance.

Starting the Cut

When you are ready to start the cut, position the saw blade well to the waste side of the drawn line, hold the blade at a low angle and point your index finger along the blade. Make a few initial dragging strokes to get the cut established, and then proceed to make increasingly larger strokes until you are using the full length of the blade. Once the cut is underway, support the board with your knee and continue at a steady pace. If you are doing it right, the saw should be more or less at 45 degrees to the wood being cut, and you should finish up with a width of wood that has a small amount of wood to the waste side of the drawn line.

Finishing the Cut

When you are about two-thirds of the way along the length of the board, reverse the board on the horses, set the saw on the waste side of the drawn line and repeat the procedure as already described – until you meet the first cut.

ABOVE: Ripping in a vice – let the weight of the saw do the work.

ABOVE: Overhand ripping on a horse with the cut underway.

ABOVE: Overhand ripping on a bench.

Ripping in a Vice

When ripping a short plank set the wood to one side of the vice screw with a piece of waste the other side of the screw to balance. Start the cut in much the same way as already described. Don't force the pace of the "thrust" stroke as this will only leave the exit side of the wood looking ragged and torn. Simply let the weight of the saw do the work. Remember to repeatedly position the wood along the way so that the point-of-cut is always near to the vice.

Overhand Ripping on the Horse

Overhand ripping on the sawhorse is a technique of making precise and accurate short-distance cuts along the grain when you want to be ready to receive the piece that's being cut. Support and position the wood on the horse so that you can look directly down on the line of cut. Start the cut from a kneeling-on-the-floor position, and then stand up, reverse the saw so that the teeth are looking away from you and along the drawn line, and proceed to cut towards the mark.

Overhand Ripping on the Bench

Overhand ripping is a technique that traditional woodworkers claim is "easy on the back". The wood is first clamped flat-side-down to the bench so that the end to be cut is looking towards you. A few low-angle starter cuts are made with the toe of the saw pointing away, the saw is reversed so that the teeth are pointing away from your body, and then both hands are clenched around the handle to supply the thrust.

TIPS BOX

If the wood starts to chatter, then reposition it in the vice or on the horse. There should be only a short distance between the support and the point of cut. Or you can adjust your stance so as to correct the alignment of the saw. If the saw binds in the wood, then use a small wedge to open up the kerf, and/or burnish the saw blade with a wax candle.

THE CROSSCUT SAW

5 brass fixing screws

Beech handle

Taper ground blade

ABOVE: A classic crosscut saw.

Crosscut saws are designed specifically for cutting wood across the grain. If you look closely at one side of the blade, you will see that every other tooth has been filed at an angle so that it has a bevel on both edges. And, of course, you will see a reverse of this on the other side of the blade. Though there are all manner of crosscut saws, everything from huge two-man saws with a handle at both ends, to miniature saws, they all share certain features. All have the same tooth formation. All are designed primarily to cut across the grain. A typical crosscut saw is a large, general purpose, straight-backed saw about 56–66 cm (22–26 in) long with 5 points to 2.55 cm (1 in).

Stance when using a Horse

Let's say that you are trimming the ends off a plank. Bridge the wood across the horses so that the line of cut is to the right-hand side of the right-hand horse. Stand between the horses, and rest your knee on the wood so that your weight holds it securely.

Starting the Cut

Set the saw down to the waste side of the drawn line. Grip the wood with your left hand and steady the blade with your thumb

nail. Make a few careful dragging strokes with the middle-to-heel of the saw to establish the line of cut, and then finally use the full length of the saw to make the stroke.

RIGHT: Starting the cut.

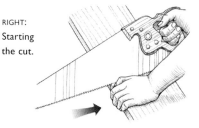

Completing the Cut

When you come to within a couple of inches of finishing the cut – when the waste end looks as if it is ready to fall away – then, simultaneously hook your left hand around the waste piece to support it and make a series of increasingly lighter strokes until the wood is sawn through.

RIGHT: Completing the cut.

ABOVE: Stance when starting the cut.

ABOVE: Raise the saw handle when the cut is underway.

ABOVE: Stance when completing the cut.

THE PANEL SAW

A panel saw is best thought of as a refined version of the general purpose crosscut. Designed for cabinet work, the smaller teeth leave a finer kerf. A popular size panel saw is 51–61 cm (20–24 in) long with about 7 points to 2.55 cm (1 in). A panel saw is a choice tool for cutting large joints at the bench.

Cutting a Panel with a Skewed Saw

1 Many traditional woodworkers favour the use of a skewed panel saw. The term "skewed" refers to the back edge of the blade being dipped or curved along its length. The combined characteristics of a 7 point cut and a skewed back add up to an exceptionally easy-to-manoeuvre tool. Generally, a skewed panel saw is lighter in weight than a straight-back.

2 The skewed feature of the panel saw reduces the stiffness of the blade so that it can be used to cut relatively full curves. The wood is supported on a pair of horses. The blade entres to the waste side of the drawn line, and then the blade is twisted and manoeuvred along the way so that it follows the curve.

TIPS BOX

There are two types of stationary power circular saws: the table or bench saw, on which the workpiece is moved over the table, and the radial-arm saw, which is pulled over the stationary workpiece. Although both saws can be used for ripping and crosscutting, the table saw is best for ripping, while the radial arm saw excels in crosscut work.

THE BACKSAW

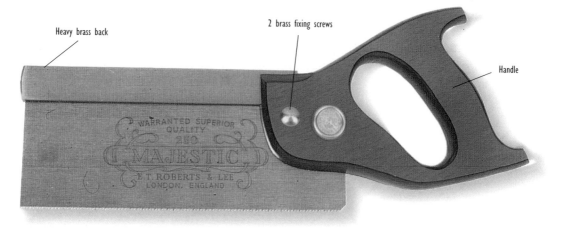

Heavy brass back

2 brass fixing screws

Handle

WARRANTED SUPERIOR
QUALITY
250
MAJESTIC
E.T. ROBERTS & LEE
LONDON. ENGLAND

ABOVE: A classic medium
length tenon saw.

Backsaws can be recognized by their brass or iron backs, the closed handle and the 30.5–40.65 cm (12–16 in) long blades with 12–14 points to 2.55 cm (1 in). These are choice saws for cutting joints and for general bench work.

Cutting a Lap End Joint

1 Having marked out the lines that go to make up the joint, set the wood in the vice at an angle of about 45 degrees and saw down to the shoulder mark. Turn the workpiece around in the vice and repeat the procedure for the other side of the joint.

2 When you have run a 45-degree angle kerf down to the shoulder line on both sides of the joint, then reposition the workpiece so that it is upright in the vice, and complete the cut.

3 Finally butt the workpiece hard up against a bench stop and make the shoulder cut to remove the waste.

Using a Back Saw with a Bench Hook

Secure the bench hook in the vice. With the workpiece being pushed hard up to the stop with your left hand, set the saw to the waste side of the drawn line and use the toe of the blade to make a few light dragging strokes. When you have established the cut, then use the full length of the blade to complete. If the saw is in good condition, and the workpiece is held tight, then the cut will only require the minimum of clean-up.

ABOVE: Bench hook – push the workpiece hard up against the stop.

Using a Back Saw with a Mitre Block

Having first made sure that your back saw and mitre block are compatible – meaning the saw blade is the same thickness as the slot – then clamp the block securely in the vice so that the top of the base is standing proud. Protect the base of the block with a piece of flat waste, then set the workpiece down and butt it hard up against the stop. Hold the whole works firm with your left hand, then ease the saw into the slot and proceed with the cut.

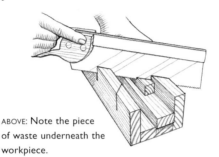

ABOVE: Note the piece of waste underneath the workpiece.

Using a Back Saw with a Sizing Board

Using a back saw in conjunction with a sizing board is the best technique for cutting short repeat lengths. The board is clamped in the vice, and the stop is adjusted for the required length. The workpiece is pushed against the back of the hook and slid to the right so that the end butts hard up against the stop. Finally, the saw is eased into the slot to make the cut.

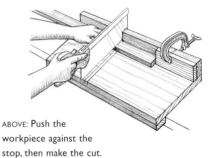

ABOVE: Push the workpiece against the stop, then make the cut.

THE GENT'S SAW

The Gent's Saw

The term "Gent's" relates to the nineteenth century when smaller "more refined" tools were designed specifically for gentlemen. This type of saw, with its turned handle, brass back and fine blade at about 25.5 cm (10 in) long with 15–20 teeth to 2.55 cm (1 in), is a good tool for cutting fine kerfs, especially on mitres and end-grain joints.

The handle is held in one hand and the toe is sometimes gripped in the other, in much the same way as when using a large rasp or plane.

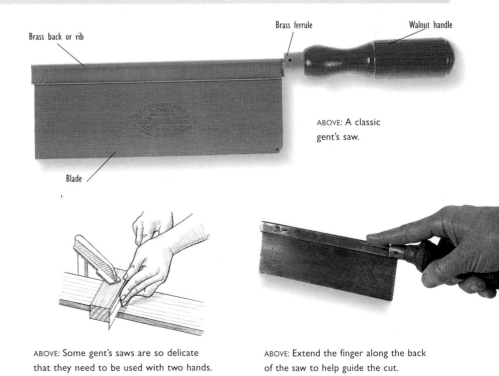

Brass back or rib

Brass ferrule

Walnut handle

Blade

ABOVE: A classic gent's saw.

ABOVE: Some gent's saws are so delicate that they need to be used with two hands.

ABOVE: Extend the finger along the back of the saw to help guide the cut.

TENON AND DOVETAIL SAWS

Brass back

Traditional shaped handle

Rip cut

ABOVE: **A** classic dovetail saw
with rip teeth, designed for use
on softer woods.

Small back saws, known variously as tenon saws and dovetail saws, are in fact small ripsaws. With a blade length of 30.5 –40.65 cm (12–16 in) and a tooth size of 12–14 points to 2.55 cm (1 in), they are designed for cutting with the grain, as when cutting tenon and dovetail joints

Cutting a Tenon

1 Secure the workpiece at a 45-degree angle in the vice. With one hand holding the saw and the other holding the workpiece and steadying the saw blade, run the line of cut down to the shoulder line. Repeat the procedure for both cuts on both sides of the joint. Then secure the wood upright in the vice, set the saw in the kerf and cut the remaining peak down to the shoulder line. Do this for both kerfs.

2 Finally, butt the workpiece hard up against the bench hook, align the saw to the waste side of the scored shoulder line so that the teeth just skim the line and cut down to the cheek.

ABOVE: The handle of the dovetail saw is designed for maximum comfort. The notch at the top of the handle enables the woodworker to point and hook his index finger for optimum control.

Sawing Dovetails

1 Having used the gauge and bevel to painstakingly mark in the shape of the dovetails on the tail board, then use a pencil to carefully shade in the areas of waste that need to be cut away.

2 Secure the workpiece in the vice and use the dovetail saw to cut down to the shoulder line. Be sure to cut to the waste side of the drawn line.

3 Secure the other board in the vice – meaning the board that has the pins and sockets. Set the sawn dovetails in place and at right angles on the end-grain face. Use the dovetail saw to transfer the lines through to the end face of the pin board. Finally, use a square to run lines down to the shoulder line.

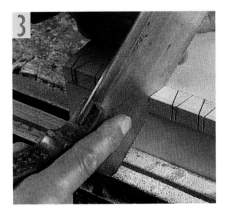

TIPS BOX

One look through a current tool catalogue will show you that there are all manner of dovetail cutting aids, from jigs and templates to router bits and complete patented systems. The best advice is to first have a go with a saw and chisel so that you know what is involved and then consider the options.

THE BEAD SAW

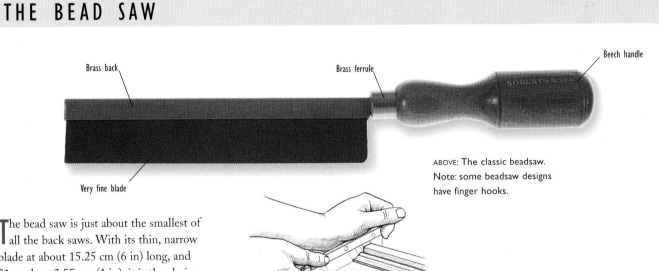

Brass back

Brass ferrule

Beech handle

Very fine blade

ABOVE: The classic beadsaw. Note: some beadsaw designs have finger hooks.

The bead saw is just about the smallest of all the back saws. With its thin, narrow blade at about 15.25 cm (6 in) long, and 21 teeth to 2.55 cm (1 in), it is the choice tool for fine, accurate work. The saw is designed to be held with both hands, one grasping the handle and supplying the push, and the other wrapped around the hook to hold the saw steady.

ABOVE: The bead saw is best held with a two-handed grip.

THE BOW SAW

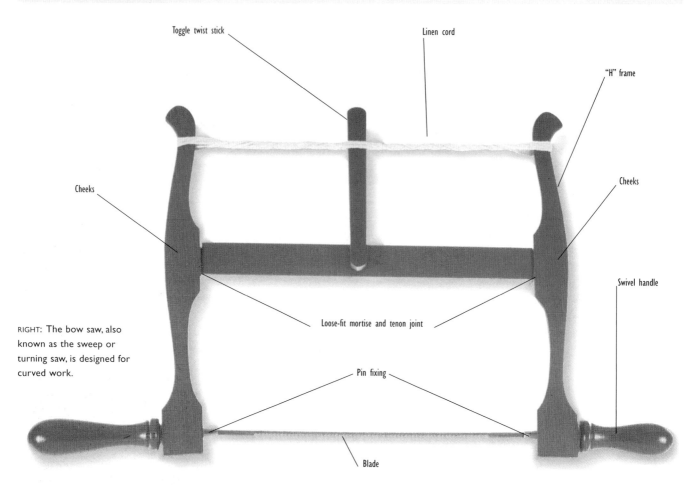

Toggle twist stick

Linen cord

"H" frame

Cheeks

Cheeks

Swivel handle

Loose-fit mortise and tenon joint

RIGHT: The bow saw, also known as the sweep or turning saw, is designed for curved work.

Pin fixing

Blade

The bow or frame saw, with its traditional wooden "H" frame and a flexible blade with about 8 points to 2.55 cm (1 in), is probably one of the most versatile of all the curve-cutting saws. The design is such that the handles can be pivoted within the frame so the saw can be set to work in any direction. The twisted cord with the toggle adjust-ment not only makes for quick blade replacement, it also allows the woodworker to keep the blade at the correct tension.

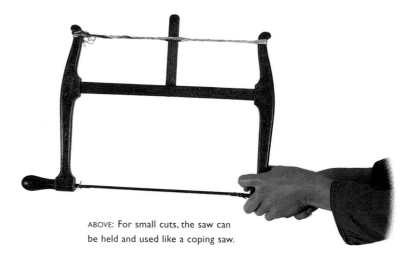

ABOVE: For small cuts, the saw can be held and used like a coping saw.

CUTTING OUT A CHAIR SEAT

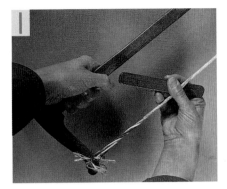

1 Twist the toggle-stick to tension the bow saw blade. Continue until the blade "pings".

2 Hold the saw upright so that it is at right angles to the face of the wood. Run a starter cut straight in towards the drawn line.

3 Hold and manoeuvre the saw with both hands, all the while bracing your body against the workpiece and turning the frame of the saw around so that it is out to the waste side of the drawn line.

4 Since the drawn line necessarily runs both with and across the grain, be ready for the rate of cut to change as you saw around the curve.

5 If you find it hard going when you come to saw directly into end grain, then you could change your approach so that you cut only with the grain.

TIPS BOX

If you are considering the power saw options, then the bandsaw ought to be well up on your list. It's good for rough-cutting wood for the lathe; it's good for cutting curves; it's great for ripping and crosscutting. And just in case you don't know already, use wide blades for straight cuts and thin blades for curves.

THE FRET SAW

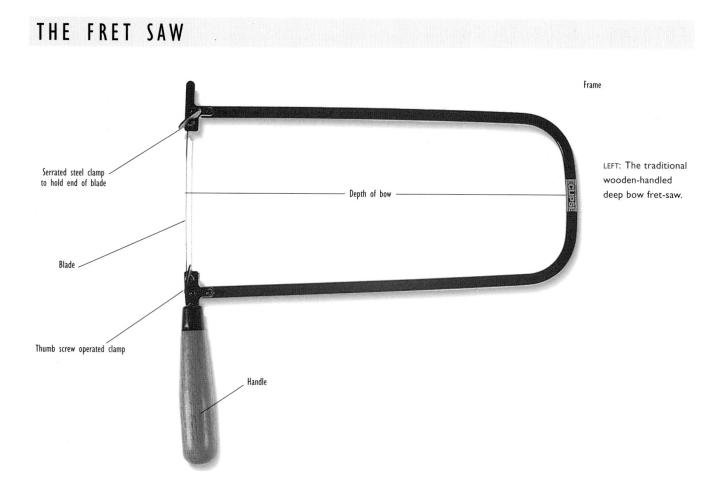

Frame

Serrated steel clamp
to hold end of blade

Depth of bow

Blade

Thumb screw operated clamp

Handle

LEFT: The traditional
wooden-handled
deep bow fret-saw.

The fret saw's bow-shaped frame and thin blade make it just perfect for cutting out intricate curved designs in thin wood. If you want to cut out pierced holes, make a jigsaw puzzle or build small table-top toys, then this is the tool for you.

ABOVE: Holding the
fret saw.

Using a Fret Saw

The blade is fitted in the frame with a couple of thumb-screws, with the frame itself having enough spring to keep the blade under tension. To install a new blade, use your body to push the frame against the side of the bench until the old blade goes slack and drops out. Then set the ends of the new blade in the little clamps, tighten up the thumbscrews and let the frame spring back.

In use, you set the workpiece in the vice, or clamp it face down so that it overhangs the bench, and then you work with a delicate push-and-pull action. Most woodworkers prefer to mount the blade so the teeth will be pointing towards the handle. That way they cut on the pull stroke, offering better contol for cutting thin wood.

ABOVE: Many woodworkers
prefer to use a bird's mouth
V-board in conjunction with
the fret saw.

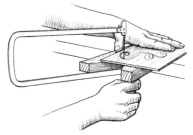

ABOVE: Holding and using the fret saw.

TIPS BOX

If you plan to make items that contain a lot of curved profiles and pierced holes – like small toys, chair backs, small boxes and the like – then the electric scroll saw is a good option. Many woodworkers go for using the electric scroll saw for cutting out overall profiles and then turn to the hand fret saw for cutting out the more delicate pierced "windows".

FRETTING A CHAIR SPLAT

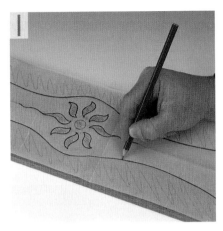

1 Having drawn up the profile and established the "windows" of the design, take a tracing and pencil-press transfer the traced lines through to the wood.

2 Drill 32 mm (1/8-in) diameter pilot holes through each of the enclosed windows. Use either the power saw or the handsaw to cut out the overall profile.

3 Finally, having secured the workpiece in the vice, take the fret saw, disconnect one end of the blade, pass the blade end through one of the pilot holes, reattach the blade and then set to work fretting out the enclosed area of waste. Repeat this procedure for all the pierced areas of the design.

BELOW: The bow-back chair with the splat in place.

TIPS BOX

The secret of using the fret saw has to do with being able to change the direction of the cut at tight angles without breaking the blade or friction-burning the wood. The correct procedure is to run the line of cut up to the angle and then at the same time increase the rate of the stroke while realigning the frame so that the blade is following the new route.

THE COPING SAW

RIGHT: Traditional wooden-handle coping saw.

Frame

Swivelling blade holders

Wooden handle that can be turned to redirect and tension the blade

The coping saw is designed for quick tight curves in wood up to about 1.25cm (½ in) thick. If you want to cut out an intricate shape or maybe an enclosed "window", then this is the tool for the job. The thin flexible blades can be replaced quickly, simply by unscrewing the handle to release the tension. The whole idea is that you use the blades until they become dull or slack and then throw them away. If you plan to make small fancy items like toys, then this is a choice tool.

ABOVE: Holding and using the coping saw.

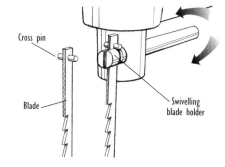

Cross pin

Blade

Swivelling blade holder

ABOVE: Close up of swivel spigot and blade.

Cutting Dovetails with a Coping Saw

1 Used as a follow-up to the dovetail saw, the coping saw is an efficient and easy-to-use tool for clearing the waste in and around the dovetails and pins. But first use the dovetail saw to establish all the straight primary cuts

2 Take the coping saw, making sure that the blade is fitted with the teeth pointing away from the handle, and then slowly tighten the blade tension until the blade "pings" when plucked. It is preferable to cut on the "push" stroke when cutting a dovetail in a vice

3 Slide the blade down to the bottom of one or other of the primary straight cuts, as made by the dovetail saw, and then work with a steady stroke to cut across the neck of waste. Be sure to keep well to the waste side of the drawn line.

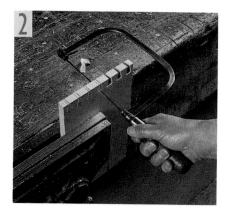

THE COMPASS SAW

Blade tapers to a slender point for curved work

Use heel of blade for heavy work

ABOVE: A modern compass saw with a tapered blade and coarse teeth.

The compass saw is designed to cut tight curves and to clear the waste from pierced areas. With a blade at about 20.3 cm (8 in) long and with around 10 points to 2.55 cm (1 in), it is a good saw for working with wood up to about 2.55cm (1 in) thick. However, the kerf tends to be so coarse and ragged that it is best to stay well to the waste side of the drawn line.

TIPS BOX

The hand-held power jig saw or reciprocating saber saw is a good option if you want to cut out curved profiles in plywood or particle board or thick sections in rough wood.

THE PAD SAW

Smaller than the compass saw, with a much thinner more flexible blade, the pad or keyhole saw is perfect for cutting small enclosed holes like holes in work surfaces, holes in doors and, of course, large keyholes. The pointed toe of the blade is introduced into the pilot hole, and the cut is initiated with a series of small strokes. Use the full length of the blade for straight cuts and the narrow end for tight curves.

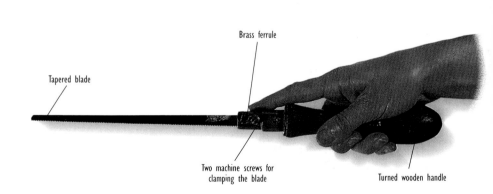

Brass ferrule

Tapered blade

Two machine screws for clamping the blade

Turned wooden handle

ABOVE: The classic compass saw.

Paring

Paring techniques form a crucial part of hand tool woodwork. Paring is the act of using chisels, gouges and knives to cut joints and otherwise shape wood. The paring procedure is very different from planing in that the woodworker is able to exert a fair degree of individual control and skill over the tool being worked. As woodworking is made up from a whole range of paring techniques, it is well worth making a collection of individual chisels, gouges and knives.

HOW CHISELS WORK

Chisels

A traditional chisel is a flat-bladed hand tool that is made up of a long, straight blade that has a cutting edge on one end and a wooden or plastic handle on the other. It can be held in one hand and pushed with the other, or it can be held in one hand and banged with a mallet. Whichever way it is held, the straight blade directs all the energy down through to the cutting edge so that the chisel cuts with a paring or shearing stroke.

Though the overall concept of the chisel remains the same, there are all manner of chisel types, each designed for a specific task. For example, a chisel with a massive handle and a thick blade is designed to be struck with a mallet, while a chisel with a delicate handle, a slender blade, a fine-angled cutting edge and with the sides of blade bevelled is designed for sensitive, two-handed use. A chisel 61 cm (24 in) or more long with a lead-weighted pommel at the butt end of the handle and with a bevel on both sides of the blade is designed for woodturning. If you are new to woodwork, then it's important to understand your needs – the tools and techniques – before you spend money on a whole collection of chisels.

Bevel Angle

If you look at the business end of a correctly ground and honed chisel blade, you will see

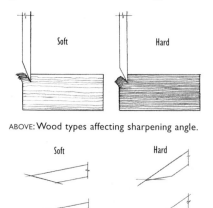

ABOVE: Wood types affecting sharpening angle.

ABOVE: Removing only a small amount of metal.

that there is an overall bevel angle, which is called a primary bevel. If you turn the blade this way and that so that it catches the light, you will see that at about 16 mm ($^1/_{16}$ in) from the cutting edge, there is a secondary bevel. The idea of the two bevels is that the primary bevel sets the angle for grinding without the need to remove too much metal, and then the secondary bevel – achieved at the honing stage – is the fine-tuned cutting edge.

Bevel Shape

The overall shape and angle of the bevel depends on the chisel's use. A big angle that rounds over into the back is for deep chopping into hardwood. A big bevel is best for paring dense, hard wood, while a small angle works better for paring soft wood. The need is always to obtain a mix of strength and cutting efficiency. Yes, a fine angle will cut hard wood, but for how long and at what cost to the bevel?

SHARPENING AND HONING

ABOVE: Japanese waterstones – single grit for general sharpening.

If your chisel or gouge is blunt or has a damaged edge, then it needs to be resharpened. Good sharpening follows this sequence: first, establish the primary bevel on the grindstone, then hone the secondary bevel on a whetstone or slip and finally remove the fine bevel – called a "wire" – on a leather strop. It's easy enough to grind chisels and straight gouges, but honing a spoon gouge needs a bit of explaining.

Honing a Spoonbit Gouge

1 One of the best ways of honing a gouge requires first taking the flat stone in one hand and the tool in the other. Hold them up to the light and then, at the same time, stroke the bevel and roll the tool so that the whole curve comes into contact with the whetstone.

2 Once you have honed the outside bevel, take an appropriately-shaped slip stone, dribble a small amount of oil on the slip and then rest the slip in the inside curve to burnish the tool to a polished finish.

3 Finally, use a fold of leather to strop both the inside and outside edges of the bevel.

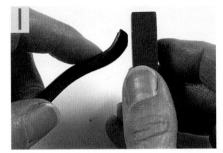

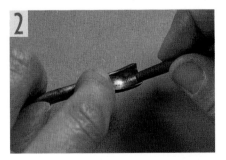

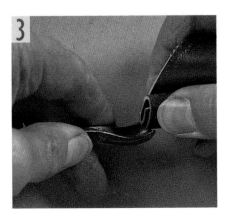

ABOVE: Diamond bench whetstone.

ABOVE: Shaped oil stone – used for sharpening woodcarving gouges.

ABOVE: One of the slip stones from a set of two.

MORTISE CHISELS

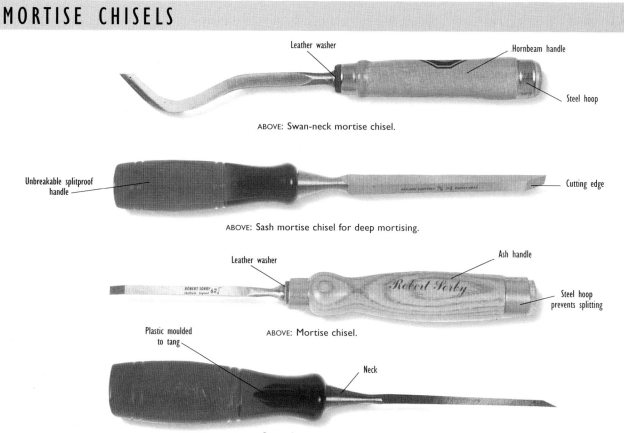

Leather washer

Hornbeam handle

Steel hoop

ABOVE: Swan-neck mortise chisel.

Unbreakable splitproof handle

Cutting edge

ABOVE: Sash mortise chisel for deep mortising.

Leather washer

Ash handle

Steel hoop prevents splitting

ABOVE: Mortise chisel.

Plastic moulded to tang

Neck

ABOVE: General purpose mortise chisel.

Mortise chisels are, as the name suggests, used primarily for chopping mortises and holes. With a heavy blade, solid wooden handle, a leather washer between the handle and shoulder and/or between the tang or socket, and sometimes also with an iron ferrule around the end of the handle, they are designed for heavy work. The handle can take repeated blows of the mallet, the leather washer deadens the blows like a shock absorber, and the heavy section of the blade means that the tool can be wrenched and levered without ill effect. There are four main types of mortise chisels: the joiner's, the sash, the registered and the swan neck.

Be careful not to damage edges

LEFT: Remove the waste with a series of backing-up cuts. Note that the bevel is on the underside.

Joiner's Mortise Chisel

With a thick blade and a heavy wooden handle, this chisel is designed primarily for chopping wide and deep mortises. It is really good for cutting large holes in hardwood.

Sash Mortise Chisel

With its narrow blade and relatively delicate wooden handle, this chisel is designed for light work such as small holes in easy-to-cut softwood.

Registered Mortise Chisel

With a flat blade and a wooden handle that has a ferrule on the butt end, this chisel – sometimes also called an "extra heavy mortise chisel" – is designed specifically for cutting hardwood.

Swan Neck Mortise Chisel

With a thick, socketed blade, a hooked swan neck and a wooden handle, this chisel is designed for chopping lock mortises in the edge of heavy security doors, cutting a deep hole into which the lock is fitted. The swan neck is designed to cut and scoop out the end grain of the cross rail tenon.

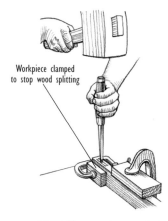

Workpiece clamped to stop wood splitting

ABOVE: Always make sure that the workpiece is well secured.

CUTTING A MORTISE

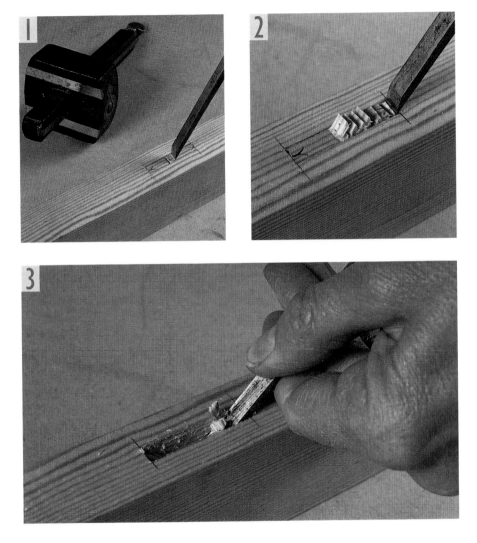

Cutting a Mortise

1 First, use a pencil, ruler, square and gauge to mark out the mortise, and then clamp the workpiece so that it is flat-down on the work surface. Take the mallet and chisel and start by cutting a small V-shaped notch at the centre of the mortise.

2 Stand to one end of the workpiece, set the chisel at the centre so that the bevel is looking away from you and then back up with the chisel. Make sure along the way that the cuts are progressively deeper and at about 65 mm (¼-in) intervals. Work to within about 16 mm (¹⁄₁₆ in) of the end, and then reverse the chisel and repeat the procedure for the other end.

3 Finally, when you have worked down to the required depth for a blind mortise, or turned the workpiece over and repeated the procedure from the other side for a through mortise, put down the mallet and clean up the ends with a few crisp paring strokes. The final paring cuts will clean up the rough ends left by the levering.

JOINTING MALLET

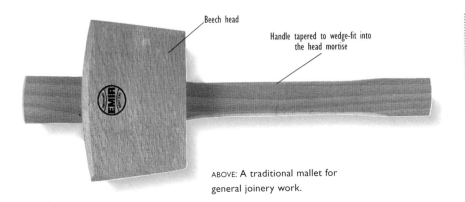

Beech head

Handle tapered to wedge-fit into the head mortise

ABOVE: A traditional mallet for general joinery work.

TIPS BOX

Though there are many techniques for cutting a mortise, the one constant is that you stay away from the ends of the mortise until the final stage, at which time you use paring cuts to clean up the damage caused by the levering action. Remember, most beginners make the mistake of cutting the mortise too large.

BEVELLED EDGE CHISELS

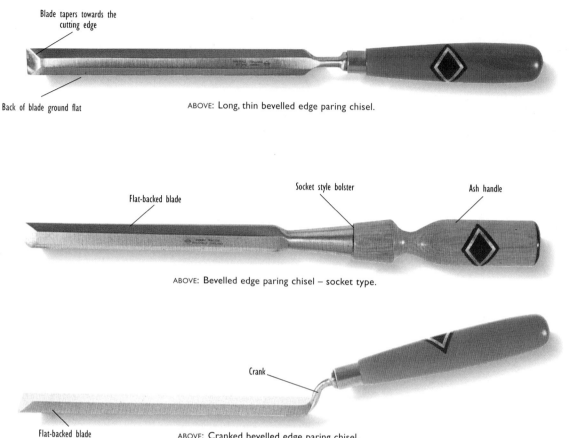

Blade tapers towards the cutting edge

Back of blade ground flat

ABOVE: Long, thin bevelled edge paring chisel.

Flat-backed blade

Socket style bolster

Ash handle

ABOVE: Bevelled edge paring chisel – socket type.

Crank

Flat-backed blade

ABOVE: Cranked bevelled edge paring chisel.

The bevelled edge chisel, sometimes also called the bevelled edge firmer and the paring chisel, is much the same as the straight-sided, general purpose chisel, except that the top face of the blade is bevelled along both sides. In use, it is designed to be held in one hand and pushed with the other. The bevelled edges allow the chisel to be used to pare out difficult-to-reach angles, as in undercut joints like sliding dovetails and housings.

If you are a beginner looking to get a good all-round chisel, one that you are certainly going to use, then the bevelled edge chisel is a good bet. There are many choices of design: ones with plastic handles, ones with the handle set in a socket, Japanese types with bevelled blades that are triangular in section, and all the

LEFT: The shape of the bevelled edge chisel allows you to clean out an undercut – as with this dovetail housing.

rest. If you are looking for a choice tool and one made in the western tradition, then you can't go wrong with a chisel that has an octagonal boxwood "London Pattern" handle, a long blade and a leather washer between the bolster and the handle. Though the bevelled edge chisel will stand

up to a small amount of light mallet tapping, it is primarily a two-handed paring tool designed for delicate joints rather than heavy carpentry. In use, it is held, pushed and manoeuvred with one hand, while at the same time being steadied, braced and aligned with the other.

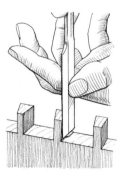

LEFT: Making a delicate paring stroke with a bevelled edge chisel.

USING A TROWEL-SHANKED BEVELLED EDGE CHISEL

Trowel-shank bevelled edge chisels – also known as crank-necked cabinet or pattern-maker's chisels – are different from their straight-shanked buddies only in the shape of the neck, which comes out at an angle so that the handle is offset – like a trowel. These chisels are designed specifically for clearing shallow housing channels or grooves in wide, thin boards. They are worked with a sliding or shearing stroke: the handle is pushed and manoeuvred with one hand, while the blade is held flat-down and aligned with the index fingers of the other hand. If you are doing it right, you will find that you are able to clear the ground without the fingers of your pushing hand getting bruised or being in the way. Remember that the trowel-shanked chisel is generally needed only when the channel is running across a board that is wider than the blade-length of your regular chisel or when it is not convenient to use a plane.

CUTTING A SLIDING HALF-DOVETAIL

1 First use a pencil, ruler and square to lay out the half-dovetail, then shade in the waste so as to avoid mistakes and use the square and marking knife to precisely establish the position of the line of cut.

2 Take a small back saw, set it down so that the thickness of the blade is to the waste side of the marked line, and then saw a kerf down to within about 16 mm (¹/₁₆ in) of the angle at the neck of the dovetail. Be careful not to hold the saw askew and not to cut past the angle.

3 With the workpiece clamped flat-down on the bench – so that you can approach it from the end – take the bevelled edge chisel and slice in from the end of the grain. If you are going at it right, then you will be cutting downhill through the run of the grain.

4 Finally, take the chisel, hold it at a low, flat angle so that it is parallel with the face of the dovetail and clean up the face and the angle. If needs be, use a guide block set at the same angle as the face of the dovetail so that you can use it to support the blade of the chisel when you are doing the final smoothing. Work the wood from both sides towards the middle so as to avoid tool-exit damage.

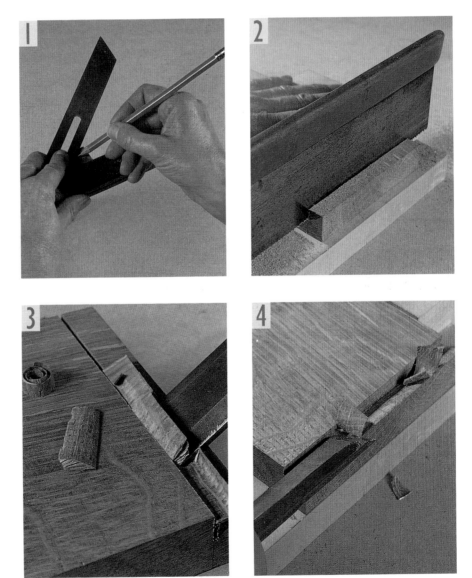

WOODCARVING GOUGES

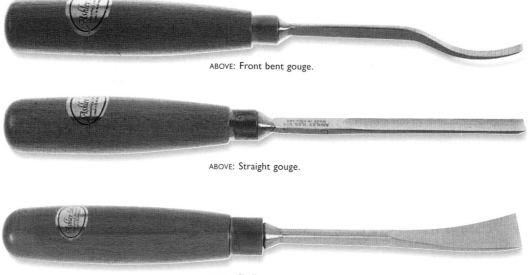

ABOVE: Front bent gouge.

ABOVE: Straight gouge.

ABOVE: Shallow sweep
front bent gouge.

The straight gouge is like a straight firmer chisel except that the gouge blade is hollowed in cross section along its length, while the chisel is flat. All gouges are designed to make a curved cut. Put another way, if you set the cutting edge of a chisel down on the wood and give it a tap, it makes a straight, dash-shaped cut, whereas if you repeat the procedure with a gouge, you get a curved cut like a "C" or "U".

When gouges are defined as being "straight", "curved", "bent" or "spoon", this simply describes the shape of the blade along its length. The combination of the shape and width of the blade in cross-section and the shape of the blade in its length results in a tool designed to do a specific task. For example, if we take three tools, a 1.2 cm (½-in)-wide straight gouge, a 1.2 cm (½-in)-wide bent gouge and a 1.2 cm (½-in)-wide spoon gouge – all with the same sweep or depth of curve at the cutting edge – they all make the same cut. But from tool to tool, the shape of the handle along its length allows the tool to variously reach, dig, scoop, pare or otherwise perform a task that is unique to itself. To put it yet another way, when you find that

a straight gouge can't be used to scoop out a cavity, then you go for a spoon bent gouge.

In use, straight gouges are held in both hands and pushed, or held in one hand and struck with the mallet. Bent, curved and spoon gouges are generally pushed and levered. If you are a beginner to woodwork and want to try your hand at woodcarving, then the best idea is to get yourself an easy-to-carve wood like basswood and just a couple of tools – say a 1.2 cm (½-in)-wide shallow U-curve straight gouge, and a 1.2 cm (½-in)-wide deep U-curve spoon gouge. You can get more specific gouge types when you understand your needs.

If you are a raw beginner and don't yet know how to sharpen your tools, then it's a good idea to buy tools that are "fully honed ready-to-use".

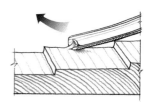

ABOVE: Bent gouge.

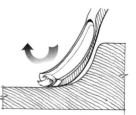

ABOVE: Spoon bit gouge.

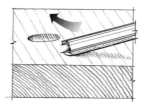

ABOVE: Straight gouge.

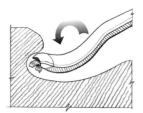

ABOVE: Back bent gouge.

CARVING MALLETS

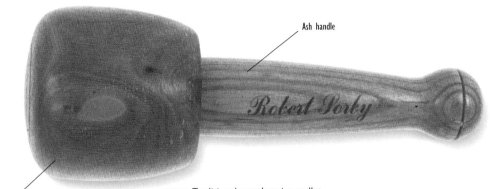

Ash handle

Lignum vitae head

ABOVE: Traditional woodcarving mallet.

Woodcarving mallets come in many shapes and sizes, everything from carefully shaped billets of wood bound around with rawhide, through to very fancy items made variously from brass, ebony, and lignum vitae. The carver's mallet is designed so that it can be easily held and controlled without the need for the carver to worry about the impact angle (the angle that the face of the mallet meets the tool). In use, the workpiece is secured in the vice or clamped to the bench, the gouge is held and directed with one hand and the mallet is swung with the other. The idea is not to make big heavy blows as with a hammer, but rather to tap-tap-tap with the mallet, while at the same time guiding and manoeuvring the gouge. The mallet is never used to deliver a single smashing blow. Use a little-by-little approach like a woodpecker, and you won't go far wrong.

A mallet needs to be carefully selected for weight, grip and size. The handle needs to be shaped for optimum comfort, there needs to be a swelling at the end of the handle so that the carver can work with a loose grip, and the weight of the head needs to be balanced to suit the individual strength and muscle power of the user.

LEFT: Tap with the mallet while manoeuvring the gouge.

Traditional Mallet

The traditional woodcarver's mallet as used in the west has a lignum vitae head and a beech handle, with the head weighing 340–850 gm (12–30 oz). Designed to be used with a series of short repeated strokes rather than single blows, the round head allows the carver to rapidly change the direction of the stroke and his hold on the gouge without worrying about how the face of the mallet is angled to the tool.

Rawhide Mallet

Designed primarily as a metal-shaping tool, the rawhide mallet is favoured by woodcarvers who have taken to using a lightweight mallet instead of doing heavy pushing with their hands. The idea is, that this mallet can be used in conjunction with relatively delicate gouges without fear of doing damage to the gouge handles. The lightweight mallet is particularly useful, when working with bent and spoon gouges, because it can be used with a light, tapping action without the woodcarver really feeling the strain of holding a heavier tool.

Rubber-head Mallet

Many woodcarvers – especially older carvers who are working day in and day out and are worried about repetitve stress injury – now favour using the soft-headed rubber or urethane mallet. They have a good-to-hold shaped wooden handle with the pommel and the same rounded head, but the resilient head does the job without the force of the impact travelling up the arm to do damage to the wrist and/or elbow. Better yet, these mallets can be dropped and generally abused without damage. Such mallets come in three head sizes and three weights.

TIPS BOX

There are basically two types of power carving tools: those that cut with a rotary action – like holding a sanding head in a drill – and those that work with a reciprocating action – like a fast vibrating pecking. Many woodcarvers claim that the small rotary tools are wonderful for fine detailing in hard wood, while the reciprocating type are great for roughing out massive carving when there is a lot of waste to be cut away.

WOODCARVING IN RELIEF

Woodcarving in relief is a technique of using gouges and chisels to variously incise, cut, excavate and model the surface of the wood to a relatively shallow depth. The technique involves drawing the pattern or design out on the wood, edging the design with a V-section trench, making decisions as to the various levels of the design and then wasting areas in and around the design with gouges.

Depending upon the design, the imagery can be seen as the areas that are cut away or as the areas that are left standing proud or a combination of the two. The terms "low" and "high" relief describe the depth of the design. For example, if the image of a flower is carved so that the area around the flower is simply lowered so that both the flower and the ground are no more than flat faced but at different levels, then this is described as low relief. If the ground is first lowered so that the flower is left standing proud and then the flower and the surrounding ground are modelled with petals, fronds and the like, then this is high relief. And of course, if we take the technique a little further and undercut both the flower and the fronds so that the flower is undercut and the fronds are in some part separate from the ground, then this is described as deep relief and pierced. Generally speaking, relief carvings are designed to be seen front on, like a picture.

1 Use the mallet and large sweep straight gouge to remove the waste. Go at it slowly, stopping regularly to see how the whole carving looks. If need be, change to a smaller gouge size.

2 When you have cleared the bulk of the waste from in and around the leaves so that the various details stand proud like plateaus, use the gouge of your choice to shape the details.

3 Having partially shaped and dished the foliage, start to model the undercuts, creating the illusion that the leaves variously curl and fold over each other.

LEFT: The finished mask —
stained, brushed with shellac,
waxed and toned.

CARVING IN THE ROUND

Carving in the round or sculptural carving is the next logical developmental step after relief carving. It is a technique in which the carver cuts deeper and deeper into the wood until the resultant carving is free standing so that it can be viewed from all angles. In reality, the carver doesn't usually go for the deeper and deeper approach, but rather he/she goes straight in and swiftly clears the rough with whatever tools seem appropriate – a saw, an axe, an adze or whatever. Then finally the carver uses the gouges for roughing out and modelling. To carve a life-size head, for example, the procedure might go: draw the front view out on the wood, use a bow saw to cut out the shape as seen in that view, repeat the procedure for the side and the top views, and finally use the gouges to carve and model. Most woodcarvers start by building a maquette of the image, and then use callipers and dividers to transfer the sizes and proportions to the workpiece. All that said, sculptural carving is still primarily a technique that uses gouges and chisel to cut the wood.

1 After using the bow/band saw to cut the image out in one view, take a small saw and work around the blank by running a series of side-by-side cuts up to the drawn line.

2 Set the workpiece in the vice, and use a good-size straight chisel to carve what you consider is the essential form. Remember that you always need to cut with the grain, from high to low wood.

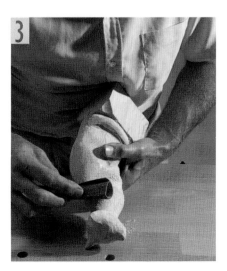

3 Use the whole range of files, rifflers and abrasive papers to work the form down to what you consider is a fine finish.

ABOVE: The finished carving is waxed and burnished to a slick finish, one that says "cat".

WOODTURNING CHISELS AND SCRAPERS

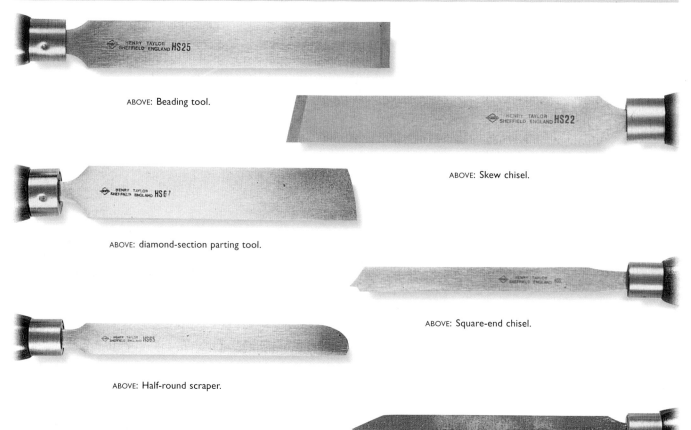

ABOVE: Beading tool.

ABOVE: Skew chisel.

ABOVE: diamond-section parting tool.

ABOVE: Square-end chisel.

ABOVE: Half-round scraper.

ABOVE: Compound-curve scraper.

Woodturning chisels and scrapers are flat-bladed tools designed specifically to be used with a woodturning lathe. The chisel has a bevel on both faces and is designed to remove the wood with a cutting action, while the scraper has a bevel on the edge and is designed to remove the wood with a scraping action. Within the two basic types, there are all manner of shapes and crosssections that are designed to make individual cuts.

Turning with Chisels

There are basically three types of cutting chisels: the square end, the skew end and the parting tool. The square end is used for general shaping, the skew chisel is used for detailed work like cutting grooves and shaping curves, and the parting tool is used primarily for parting the finished workpiece off from the waste. In use, the chisel is held in both hands and set down on the T-rest so that one hand is holding the handle while the other is gripping the blade knuckles up. The bevel is brought up to the spinning workpiece and then, simultaneously, the handle is lowered and manoeuvred so the cutting edge is advanced to the left or right along the workpiece. If the tool is well braced to resist the upward thrust of the workpiece, then the levering movement on the T-rest fulcrum results in the blade removing the waste in a slicing or paring action. If you are doing it right, the waste will spill off as continuous ribbons of shavings.

Turning with Scrapers

Most beginners to woodturning tend to start out with scraper chisels for the simple reason that they are so easy to use. After first using a gouge to turn the wood down to a clean round section, the scraper is held flat down on the tool rest with the cutting edge held level with the centre of the work, and then it is advanced in much the same way as when using the chisel. The main difference – the reason why scrapers are the beginner's first choice – is that it's very difficult to make a mistake. Certainly the scraped finish isn't as clean as a cut finish, but from the beginner's viewpoint it does at least get them there. Old tool catalogues show boxed sets of 100 different scrapers – each and every one of them designed to cut a particular profile.

WOODTURNING GOUGES

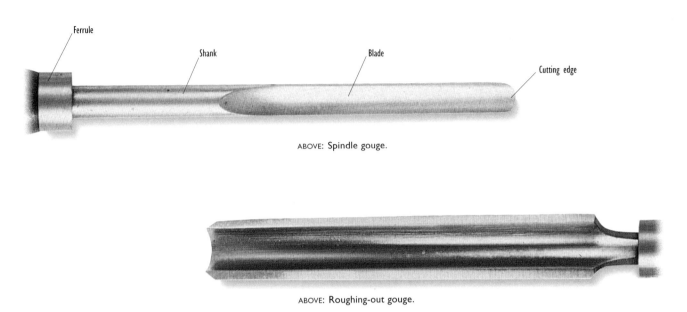

Ferrule

Shank

Blade

Cutting edge

ABOVE: Spindle gouge.

ABOVE: Roughing-out gouge.

Woodturning gouges are U-section tools that have a bevel on the outside convex edge. Though gouges come in various lengths and section sizes, with all manner of handle lengths, weights and profiles, there are, in fact, two types: the square-ended, which is ground straight across at the cutting edge, and the round-ended or round-nosed, which is rounded at the cutting edge.

Using the Roughing-out Gouge

The square-ended roughing-out gouge is the essential tool for working between centres.

Coming in two common width sizes 1.9 cm (³/₄ in) and 9.18 cm (1-¹/₄ in), this is the tool to use at the start of the project when you need to quickly size the square block of wood down to a round section. In use, the tool is set down on the T-rest so that it is at right angles to the workpiece. Then it is advanced so that it comes into contact with the spinning wood. Next it is twisted slightly to one side or the other so that the side of the U-section is looking in the direction of the cut, and then the tool is run along the wood. The best way to learn the technique, is to mount a piece of

5 cm (2-in), square-section wood between centres and to try it out.

Using the Round-Nosed Gouge

The round-nosed gouge comes in the same size and section as the square-nosed gouge. The only difference is that the cutting edge is rounded rather than square. This is the tool to use for run-of-the-mill hollow work-like spindles and bowls. The tool is set down on the T-rest, advanced and manoeuvred in much the same way as the square-ended gouge, but this tool is much easier to use. There are no corners to dig in and damage the workpiece. In fact, many beginners to woodturning start out by grinding the square-ended gouges down to a round nose, and then they grind them back to square when they get the hang of things.

Using the Deep-long-and-strong Gouge

The deep-long-and-strong gouge is the perfect gouge for turning deep-curved

spindles and bowls. It is much the same as the ordinary gouge except that it is rounder in cross-section – more like a cylindrical bar – with the bevel ground at a short angle. The advantage of the long-and-strong gouge is that the cutting edge can be a good distance away from the tool rest without worrying about vibration. The long-and-strong gouge is usually held with the handle well down and the bevel resting on the workpiece.

TIPS BOX

Both to cut costs and to achieve maximum control by minimizing vibration and judder, some woodturners purchase the long-and-strong gouge unhandled. Then they can make their own much longer handle that is lead-weighted at the pommel end. The weighted end of the handle is supported low down on the outside thigh.

TURNING A CHAIR LEG SPINDLE

Turning a traditional Windsor-type chair leg is one of those almost magical techniques that every beginner wants to try. It is a wonderful thing to see a chair-leg bodger at work. One moment the workpiece is no more than a rough billet of green wood, and then, before you can say, "Windsor chairs are wonderful", a few swift passes of the gouge and a little bit of deft handling of the skew chisel has the leg roughed out, sized, rounded, decorated with beads, done-finished and off the lathe – all in about four minutes! Just think on it: One leg every four minutes means about 15 legs an hour, or 120 turned legs in an eight-hour day, or about 720 legs in a six-day week, or...

1 Use the roughing-out gouge to swiftly turn the wood down to a round section.

2 Having used the dividers to establish the various step-offs that go to make up the design, use the tool of your choice to set-in the various levels.

3 Use a large skew chisel to turn the large broad convex curves to shape.

4 Finally, having first used the finest grit sandpaper to bring the turning to a smooth finish, stand back and assess your work. If the turning needs to be waxed, now is the time to do it.

TURNING A BOWL

There is nothing quite so pleasurable in woodturning as taking a choice piece of sycamore or maybe a nice block of maple, and turning it into a shallow bowl. If the tools are sharp, and the bowl is a nice, clean-lined form, then the wood will reveal a grain that is wonderfully lustrous and dynamic. And as if that isn't pleasure enough, there is the very special am-I-talented-or-what feeling of sitting back and watching as the bowl is used at the table. And, of course, when admirers offer you cash to make more bowls, then it just gets better and better!

1 Use the gouge to clear the waste and to establish the overall profiles and steps that go to make the outside shape of the bowl.

2 When you are pleased with the outside profile and finish, reverse the bowl on the chuck. Spend time making sure that the workpiece is perfectly centred.

3 Reposition the T-rest so that you can approach the workpiece front-on. Use a parting tool to establish the width of the rim, then use the tools of your choice to hollow out the inside shape of the bowl.

4 Use the double callipers to check the thickness of the wall of the bowl.

ABOVE: A well-formed, turned bowl.

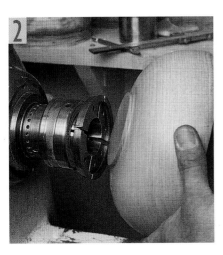

SPOKESHAVES

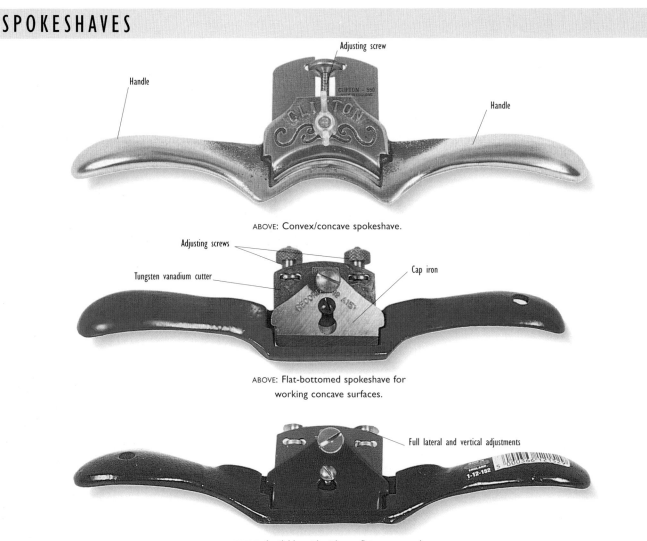

ABOVE: Convex/concave spokeshave.

Adjusting screws

Tungsten vanadium cutter

Cap iron

ABOVE: Flat-bottomed spokeshave for
working concave surfaces.

Full lateral and vertical adjustments

ABOVE: Available with either a flat or a round
base – for convex or concave work.

The spokeshave is essentially a short-soled plane with a winged handle at each side. It is designed primarily to shave and shape the edges of thin-section wood. If you need to shave the edge of a table top or sculpt the edge of a fancy curved shelf or bracket, then this is the tool for the job. The key words are "shave" and "thin wood". There are four basic forms: the traditional wooden version with a beech stock and a straight-tanged cutter; an all-metal version with a straight blade that might or might not have a screw adjustment; an all-metal version designed to shave a convex section; and an all-metal version designed to shave a concave or hollow section. The basic working procedure is to hold the spokeshave in both hands, set it across the thickness of the wood at a right angle and then push like a plane. However, in some situations, it is an advantage to skew the spokeshave across the wood so as to make a shearing or slicing cut and/or reverse the

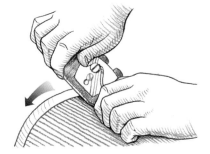

ABOVE: Following the
grain downhill.

ABOVE: It is
important that
the tool is held
at right angles to
the wood.

tool and pull it like a drawknife. No matter how the spokeshave is held, or what type you are using, the one constant is that you always work with the grain, or you might say, downhill.

SHAPING A CHAIR ARM

First, make sure that the blade is razor sharp. Spend some time adjusting the setting until the blade edge is parallel with the body of the stock or the throat. With the workpiece secured in the vice so that the edge to be worked is uppermost, take the spokeshave firmly in both hands, and brace your thumbs in the little depressions or curves in the frame at each side of the blade. Stand to one end of the workpiece so that the tool bridges the wood, and then set the tool down on the wood and draw your elbows back so that they are tucked into the sides of your waist. When you are happy with your stance, start the stroke by inching the spokeshave forwards slightly until you feel the blade begin to bite. Then straighten your arms so as to complete the stroke.

1 Start by cutting the rough-sawn faces to the level of the drawn line. Be ready to change your approach and/or the way the wood is secured so that you always cut downhill in the direction of the grain.

2 Be careful at the curved hand-hold end of the arm that you don't split off the relatively short grain.

3 Best use a wooden spokeshave to round-over the edges of the arm.

4 Continue by redrawing the guide lines, removing the waste with one or other of the shaves and reworking the lines until you have what you consider to be a fine form.

TIPS BOX

The cutter from the all-metal spokeshave is sharpened like a plane blade, while the cutter from the wooden spokeshave is sharpened like a knife. The best knife-sharpening procedure for the wooden spokeshave blade is to hold the tangs in both hands so that the bevel side is uppermost, and then to rub the bevel with a small slipstone.

KNIVES

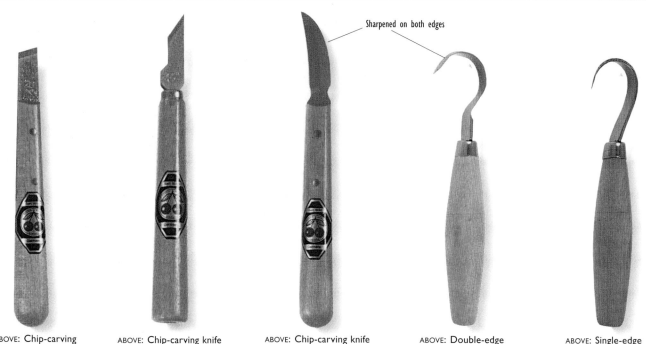

Sharpened on both edges

ABOVE: Chip-carving knife – with a straight blade and skew edge.

ABOVE: Chip-carving knife – with a skew edge.

ABOVE: Chip-carving knife – with a double-sided curved blade.

ABOVE: Double-edge hook knife.

ABOVE: Single-edge hook knife.

The knife is one of the oldest tools known to man. Whoever it was that first discovered that a flake of flint could cut wood was on to one of the biggest technological breakthroughs ever!

We all know what a knife looks like, but as for safe and efficient use, that's something again. There are about four basic holds: the grasp with the blade looking away from the body for big slicing strokes; the elbows hard into your body with both hands braced by your chest for more controlled slicing strokes; the thumb-braced levering stroke when you are cutting towards your thumb; and a thumb-push stroke for tight control when you are detailing. But what knife to use? The following directory will help you understand your options.

Chip Carving Knives

Chip carving is a pattern-making technique that involves using knives to cut triangular-shaped pockets in the surface of wood. There are three basic knife forms: the "sheepsfoot", which is characterized by having a short blade and a long handle, and is used with a pushing action; the "skew-blade", which is designed to be used like a pushing or paring chisel; and the "off-set", which is designed to make a dragging stroke.

Crooked Knife

The crooked or hooked knife, as used traditionally by the Northwest Coast Native Americans, is the choice tool for carving and whittling hollows in bowls and dishes. It is a long hook-bladed knife with a curved handle. It is gripped like a dagger so that the thumb is looking towards the end of the handle and then it is rocked and levered by the action of the thumb so that it removes waste with a scooping and hooking action.

ABOVE: A crooked knife in action.

Sheath Knife

The sheath or hunting knife with its long-single-edged blade is, in many ways, a jack-of-all-trades, or you might say it is anything that you want it to be! It is good for whittling and for splitting wood. It will sharpen dowels and tackle all the other cutting, scraping, splitting and spiking tasks that crop up in the workshop. It wins over many other knives in that the fixed, through-handle blade makes for a strong, trustworthy tool.

Hacking Knife

The traditional hacking knife, sometimes called a chipping knife, has a heavy, thick-backed through-blade and a rivetted hide handle. The tool is something more than a knife but less than an axe. In use, the blade is set down on the end grain, and the back

ABOVE: Hack knife.

of the blade is struck with a hammer. The thick hide handle cushions the blows. It's a good tool for all the rough tasks.

Jack Knife

If you are one of those woodworkers who is always on the lookout for drift wood, special sticks in the hedgerow, little sticks or crutches from the mountains and woods, then you may be looking for a good traditional fold-up pocket knife, a knife that can be used for a wide range of tasks. This is the one.

Sloyd Knife

A genuine Swedish sloyd knife is a must. Made from the famous laminated Mora steel, the blade can easily be sharpened to a razor edge. Many woodworkers, especially those who like to whittle figures, spoons, bowls and the like, claim that this knife is the best of the best.

RIGHT: A sloyd knife

Penknife

A small penknife is a joy to own and use. Small enough to slip into a side pocket, it is a wonderful tool for all the small delicate marking, skimming, whittling and trimming tasks that crop up in most workshops. Search the markets for a little two-bladed, bone-handled English knife about 10cm (4 in) long – one made before the age of stainless steel.

WHITTLING A PAN SLICE

All you need for this project is a good sharp knife and a piece of smooth-grained, easy-to-carve wood like lime wood, cherry or plum. Before you start the project, experiment with some scrap wood. If the blade cuts up rough, then either the wood is ragged and unsuitable, and/or your knife is blunt. And just in case you are a wee bit nervous – say a parent showing a child how to whittle, or a teacher with a student – then you can derive comfort from the old adage, "A dull knife is a dangerous friend". You are more likely to have an accident with a blunt knife that needs to be bullied into action than with a sharp one that does the job. As to how sharp is sharp, you ought to be able to shave the hairs on your arms with a good knife.

1 Brace the workpiece against the work surface and use big, controlled strokes to clear the bulk of the waste.

2 When you have established the overall shape of the form, use more restrained, thumb-braced paring strokes to define the details.

3 Use the two-handed stroke for a stroke-controlled cut. Link the thumbs for maxium efficiency.

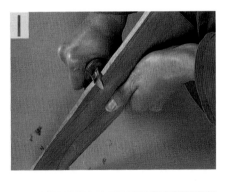

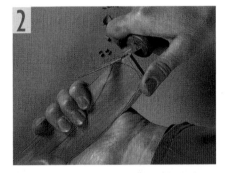

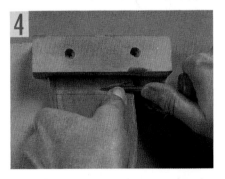

4 Butt the business end of the slice hard up against the bench hook stop and use the sharpened knife of your choice to cut the bevel.

5 Finally use a little of your favourite cooking oil to burnish the finished slice to a high sheen.

DRAWKNIVES

Blade bevelled on the outside

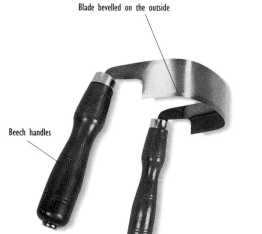

Beech handles

ABOVE: The inshave or scorp is the perfect tool for hollowing out dishes and bowls.

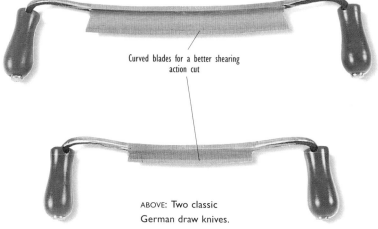

Curved blades for a better shearing action cut

ABOVE: Two classic German draw knives.

Drawknives in all their many guises are simply single-bevel blades that are fitted with a handle at each end. There are straight knives for general work, slightly curved knives that are used to skim a surface to a flat finish and the U-shaped knife – called an inshave – that is used for hollowing. The very best knives have good-to-grip, slightly splayed wooden handles that are fitted by having the tangs running through the handle and clenched over at the ends. The drawknife is a wonderfully efficient and safe tool to use.

The two-handed pulling action not only allows you to put the whole weight of your body behind the stroke but, better still, the stance with both arms held straight out from the elbows makes it almost impossible to cut yourself. If you want to make items like Windsor chairs, boat spars and large carved bowls, then you need a couple of drawknives.

Drawknife Technique

With the workpiece held securely in the vice or with a holdfast, take the drawknife in both hands so that the bevel is set down on the workpiece. Brace your feet in readiness, cock the knife at a slightly skewed angle, and then draw the knife towards your body to make a shearing or slicing cut. You will soon find that by adjusting the angle and/or putting more weight behind the cut it is possible to achieve anything from the lightest paring cut through to a deep-splitting rough cut. As for the question of which way to have the bevel facing, don't worry about the "experts" who claim that there is only one way. The general rule is: bevel down for maximum control and skimming cuts, and bevel up when you are aiming to remove great slices of waste. The inshave is used in much the same way as the straight-bladed drawknife. The only real difference is that the strokes always need to be short and slicing rather than long and deep. When you are working dished forms, you always have to work from side-to-centre so as to avoid cutting into end grain.

ABOVE: Hold the drawknife with well-braced arms, and clear the waste with a series of short, shallow slicing strokes.

ABOVE: For full and safer control, always hold the drawknife with two hands.

MAKING A GREEN WOOD CHAIR LEG

All you need for this try-out project is a length of green wood, a good sharp drawknife and a means to hold the wood while it is being worked. You will find in the beginning that the bench vice is adequate. The term "green wood" should be taken to mean wood from a fresh-cut log at about 25–35 cm (10–14 in) in diameter. The best way of getting at the wood is to use a wedge and sledge hammer to split the log down its centre, then to split the halves into quarters and so on until you have cake-wedge sections about 7.5–10cm (3–4 ins) wide across the span of the circumference arc.

1 Set the roughed-out billet in the vice so that the end to be worked is set up at a comfortable work angle.

2 Take the drawknife firmly in two hands. Set it at a skewed angle so that the bevel is looking towards the wood, and then draw it towards your body. It is best to shave a little, and then turn the wood slightly, shave a little more, and turn the wood, and so on.

3 When you have shaved one end to a round crosssection, then all you do is repeat the procedure for the other end.

ABOVE: Don't try for a looks-to-be turned finish, rather aim for a form that is confident, with fair curves.

TIPS BOX

The secret of success when using a drawknife to make stick-legs for chairs and stools, or rods for Windsor chair backs, or whatever, is to always use green wood. You will soon find out, that while seasoned wood from the lumber yard resists every cut, green wood cuts like cheese.

Planing

Hand planes are uniquely satisfying tools to use, producing instantly rewarding results of a smooth surface. Certainly electric planers are gaining popularity, and it is a fact that prepared lumber is readily available. But many woodworkers find it infinitely more rewarding to build up a stock of specialist hand planes and then to learn a whole range of traditional hand-planing techniques.

SHARPENING AND SETTING

Hand planes are uniquely satisfying tools to use, with the instantly rewarding results of a smooth surface. Most woodworkers will agree: using a well-tuned plane is one of the high spots of fine woodworking – no pun intended. However, if your plane is badly set up, with a dull cutting iron, or a cap iron with a badly bevelled edge, or it is in any way less than perfect, then it will ruin both your work and your day.

Looking at the Bench Plane Cap Iron and Cutter

Lift the cap lock and remove the lever cap. Next lift out the cap iron and cutter assembly and have a close-up look. There should be little or no gap between the leading edge of the lever cap and the top face of the cap iron. And the same goes for the leading edge of the cap iron and the top face of the cutter iron. If there is a gap, then the best thing to do, is to hone the underside of the lever cap and/or the cap iron to a flush fit. See also how the screw adjustment of the cap iron allows you to vary the gap width between the edge of the cap and the edge

of the cutter. The rougher the wood, the wider the setting. A good average for everyday work is about 32 mm ($1/8$ in).

Honing the Bench Plane Cutter

The plane iron has two bevels – the primary bevel at about 25 degrees, and the secondary bevel at 5 degrees more. This may sound a bit complicated, but in practice, it is really quite simple. First grind and hone the blade to a primary bevel angle of 25 degrees. Then you cock the blade up another 5 degrees – so that you have a total angle of 30 degrees – and run the blade on the finest stone so as to create the secondary bevel. If you look at the bevel by turning it to the light, you will see that the second honing results in secondary bevel along the leading edge of the first – shown by a thin strip of light. The function of the secondary bevel is to give the blade extra sharpness without the need to remove too much steel.

Sharpening Technique

Having said that planing is a joy, the follow-up proviso must be: "But only if the cutter is fully honed and stropped". There is nothing quite so demoralizing as trying to bully a dull-edged plane into action. The truth is that a good part of the technique of planing has to do with keeping the cutting iron sharp. And just in case you are a misguided beginner who is seeking to avoid what you consider is the chore of sharpening by getting a new plane – your thinking being that new planes are sharp and ready to use – you have got to realize that most new planes are labelled: "Honing required before use". New tools or old, it all adds up to the fact that you will need to learn how to sharpen your plane irons.

ABOVE: The lever cap must be a flush fit on the cap iron.

ABOVE: Setting the irons for rough work.

ABOVE: Setting the irons for finishing and hardwoods.

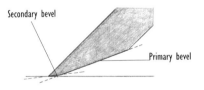

Secondary bevel

Primary bevel

ABOVE: The bevels on the cutting iron.

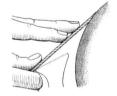

ABOVE: Grinding the primary bevel.

ABOVE: Honing the cutting edge.

The Sharpening Sequence

1 **Grinding square** – If the cutting edge is in any way nicked, then the edge will need to be squared. Set the iron bevel-up and square on the tool rest, and move it left to right across the face of the grindstone.

2 **Polishing the back** – Set the iron bevel-up and lap it on a sheet of fine grade emery cloth. Polish the back to a high-shine finish.

3 **Grinding the primary bevel** – Hold the iron bevel-down on the grinding wheel with the blade at an angle of 25 degrees, and run it from side to side.

4 **Honing the secondary bevel** – Set the blade bevel-down on the stone, cock it up at an angle that is slightly larger than the primary bevel and make several dragging passes.

5 **Stropping** – Finally, drag the bevel along the strop to remove the "wire" or waste at the cutting edge.

TIPS BOX

Woodworking gurus may be able to perfectly judge the bevel angle on their plane irons by touch and sight, but for the rest of us the best way to go is to use a grinding/honing jig or guide. These little jigs are foolproof, they cost very little and save hours of perspiration and exasperation.

THE BENCH PLANE

RIGHT: The classic metal bench plane in side view cross-section, showing how the whole tool is assembled.

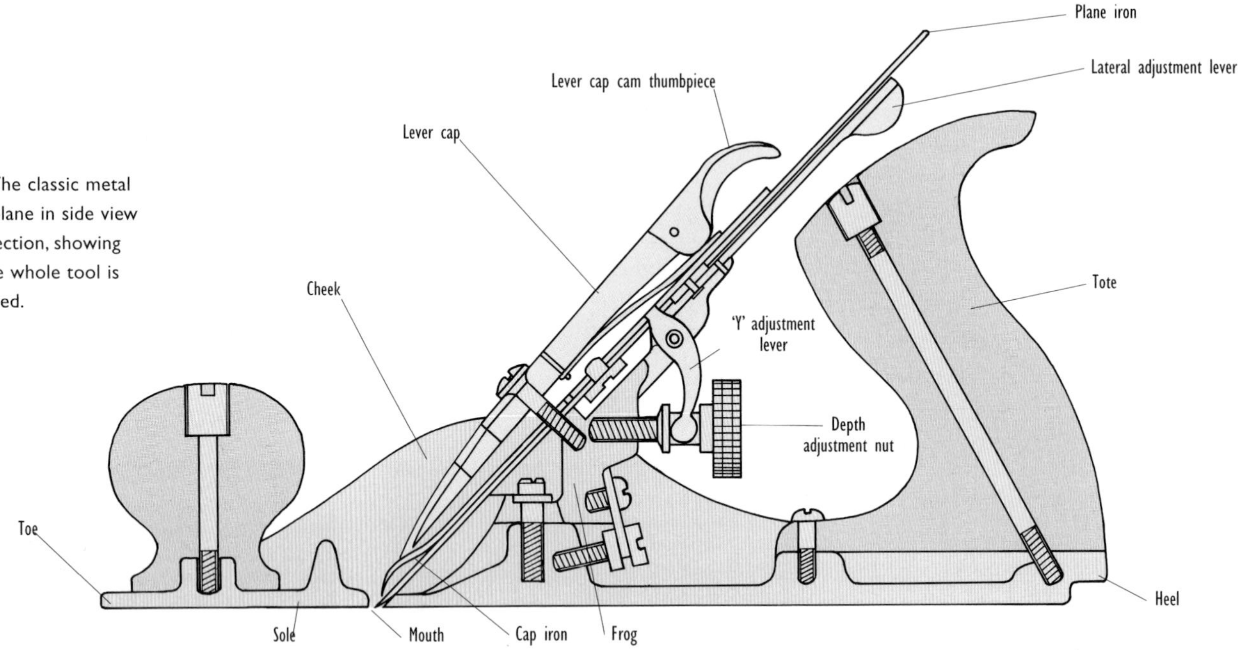

Plane iron

Lever cap cam thumbpiece

Lever cap

Lateral adjustment lever

Cheek

'Y' adjustment lever

Depth adjustment nut

Tote

Toe

Sole

Mouth

Cap iron

Frog

Heel

ABOVE: The metal bench-plane in dissassembled view.

Lever cap

Lever cap cam thumbpiece

Plane iron

TIPS BOX

The best way of finding out about your new plane is to strip it down to its component parts, and then see how they all fit and work in relation to each other.

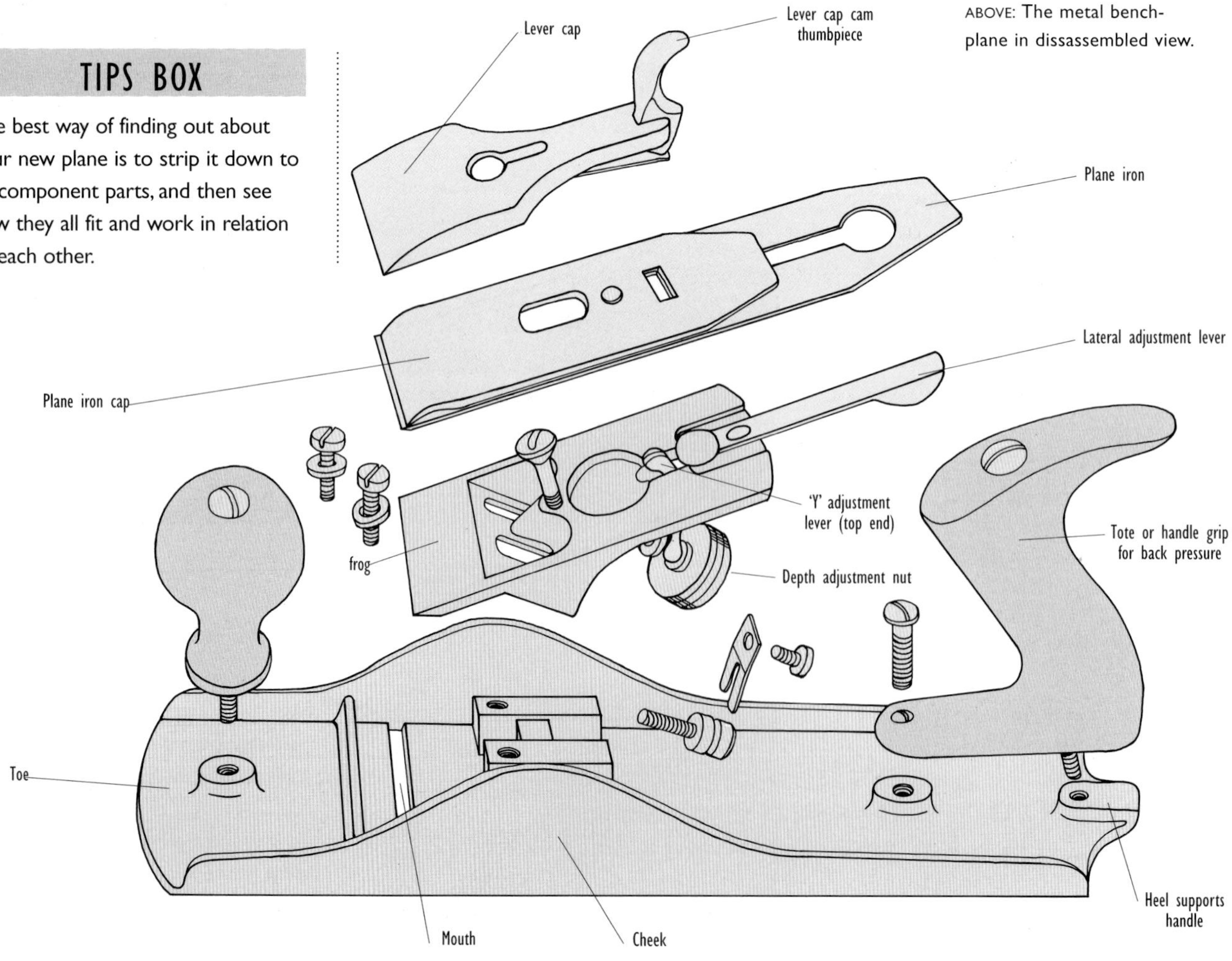

Plane iron cap

Lateral adjustment lever

frog

'Y' adjustment lever (top end)

Depth adjustment nut

Tote or handle grip for back pressure

Toe

Heel supports handle

Mouth

Cheek

Adjustment Techniques

Although the modern bench plane is a delight to use and a joy to hold and handle, it is also the most abused and misused tool in the workshop. Part of the problem has to do with the fact that there are so many moving parts and possible adjustments. The challenge is not that it's particularly difficult to adjust the depth of cut or to adjust the gap between the cap and the cutting iron or whatever, but rather the problem is how to achieve a balance of all the possible adjustments.

The following adjustment techniques will ensure that you get the best out of your plane. Start by stripping the plane down to its component parts.

Adjusting the Size of Mouth

In simple terms, big mouth equals big, greedy shavings from softwood, while a small mouth equals fine, petite shavings from hardwood. To adjust the size of the mouth set the frog in place with the three screws, and try out the adjustment screw. You will see that a clockwise turn pushes the frog forwards and makes the mouth smaller. When you have achieved a setting to suit, then tighten up the two frog screws.

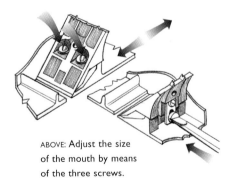

ABOVE: Adjust the size of the mouth by means of the three screws.

Adjusting the Cap and Cutter Irons

If you could take a close-up woodworm's-eye-view and watch the plane at work, you would see that the lower "cutter" iron – the one with the bevel – does the cutting, while the top "cap" iron breaks the shavings and directs them away from the throat. You would also see that the two irons need to be clamped together, so as to stop the whole works from shaking and chattering. To adjust the irons, simply undo the screw, slide the cap iron backwards or forwards and then tighten up. Allow a bigger distance between the leading edges for rough work and a smaller distance for fine work. If there is a gap between the underside of the leading edge of the cap and the cutter, then it's important that you grind the underside edge of the cap iron to a flush fit.

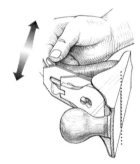

ABOVE: Move the lateral lever left or right to set the iron square in the mouth.

Adjusting the Lateral Movement

When you have adjusted the frog and the two cutters, set the cutter assembly in place so that the "dog" is engaged in the slot. Then push the lateral lever either left or right to set the cutting iron square or parallel with the mouth.

Adjusting the Depth of Cut

With the irons in place and set square to the mouth, slide the lever cap on its screw and secure the whole works with the cap lock. It needs to be tight, but not so tight that you can't make adjustments with the lateral lever and the depth wheel. The depth of cut is adjusted simply by turning the large brass wheel – clockwise for a deeper, heavier cut, and anti-clockwise for a shallow, skimming cut.

ABOVE: Adjust the depth of the cut by advancing or retracting the blade.

General Bench Plane Techniques

The bench plane is designed to be held in both hands, one hand holding and bearing down on the front knob and the other hand gripping the back handle or tote. The workpiece is secured to the bench, and the plane is set down with the left hand gripping the front knob and the right hand gripping the tote. Then the weight of the right shoulder is used to push the plane forwards. The plane should be well tuned and adjusted – with the cutter honed, all the moving parts lightly oiled and the sole burnished with a wax candle – and the wood should be carefully chosen.

That done, only three important factors in the planing procedure remain: the height of the bench, the depth of the cut, and the amount of pressure that you put down on the front of the plane. The height of the bench is something you will have to sort out to suit your own needs, but the other two considerations can be learned by trial and error. Most woodworkers start with the cutting iron set well up so that it doesn't cut, and then they repeatedly tweak the wheel very slightly clockwise and take a stroke until they are achieving the thinnest of paper-thin shavings. As to the question of how hard you should bear down on the front knob, the best way of finding out is to make test runs so that you can make a positive judgment.

THE JOINTER PLANE

Extra long sole

LEFT The jointer plane, sometimes known as a try plane, is used for truing up the edge of boards.

The jointer plane, sometimes also called a long plane, is designed specifically to prepare the edges of boards that are to be glued or otherways butted and joined together. The obvious difference between the jointer and other large planes is that the sole of the jointer is impressively long at 50–80 cm (22–36-in). The not so obvious difference is that the jointer cutter iron is ground square. The cutters of the other large planes are variously ground with a slight crown or camber, or rounded at the corners so that they can be used to face large boards without the worry about the corners of the cutter scoring the wood. Certainly you can use the other large planes for jointing and vice versa, but only if the cutters are correctly ground.

Jointing Defined

The technique of planing the edges of boards true, straight and square is termed "jointing". The object of the exercise is to create a wide board by joining one or more narrow boards edge to edge. One might ask why the woodworker shouldn't just select

BELOW: Use both hands to achieve a well-balanced stroke.

LEFT: Plane down the high spots.

a wide board.
The answer is beautifully simple: wide boards are expensive and difficult to obtain, and they tend to excessively shrink across their width, while narrow boards are relatively inexpensive, easy to obtain and offer minimal shrinkage and warping. The jointing procedure involves planing away all the high spots down to the level of the low spots and then truing up edges so that the boards can be perfectly mated edge-to-edge along their length. The long sole of the jointing plane rides on and cuts the high spots. This can be seen by the short shavings it produces. For example, if the edge has three high spots, then the plane will start by throwing up three short shavings. Of course, as the three high spots get lower and lower, so the three shavings will get longer and longer, until the joyous moment comes when the plane sends out only a single continuous shaving to signal that the edge is true.

Jointing a Single Board

To joint a single board: set the board on the bench so that one end is placed at eye level and sight down the edge. Mark the high spots or peaks with a pencil. Next, secure the board in the vice and plane off the pencil markings. Repeat this procedure

until you have what you consider is a fairly true edge. When you have cleared the obvious peaks, secure the board in the vice and use the jointer plane to plane the edge. If you work at it slowly and carefully, the jointer plane will ride very nicely on the remaining peaks so that you only skim away the remaining high spots. Finally, test the edge with straight edge and square.

Jointing a Pair of Boards

To joint a pair of boards: first set the boards down on the bench and decide how you want them to be arranged. Set the mating edges together and pencil mark the best face. Next, fold the two boards back-to-back so that the best faces are looking outwards like the cover of a book and so that the mating edges are together and uppermost, then secure them in the vice. Now run the jointer along the paired boards and plane the edges square and true. Finally, open out the "book" so that the planed edges are together. The clever thing about this technique is that if the edges are something less than square – and they nearly always are – then the "book" procedure very nicely compensates and remedies the problem.

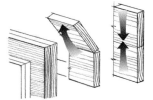

ABOVE: Jointing two boards.

Jointing Boards

The "book" technique of jointing is used when you need to butt two boards edge-to edge to make a larger board or panel. If, after jointing, the board edges are less than square, and they nearly always are, then the "book" procedure resolves the problem.

1 Secure the two boards side-by-side in the vice with the mating edges uppermost and the best faces looking outwards, then use the plane to estimate how much wood needs to be removed.

2 Run the plane along the wood, first removing the peaks of waste and then cutting down to a true square finish.

3 Remove the boards, fold them out so that the mating edges are together and the best faces are uppermost, like pages or cover of a book.

4 Once the two boards are completely opened and the edges butted together, you will see how the technique compensates for edges that are somewhat less than true.

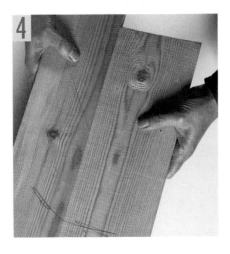

TIPS BOX

There is no doubt that an electric planer generally gets the job done faster and with less effort. However, electric planers are very noisy and dusty. If you are going to get yourself such a machine, then you must also buy the ancillary equipment like a dust collector, ear protectors and a full face shield.

THE SMOOTHING PLANE

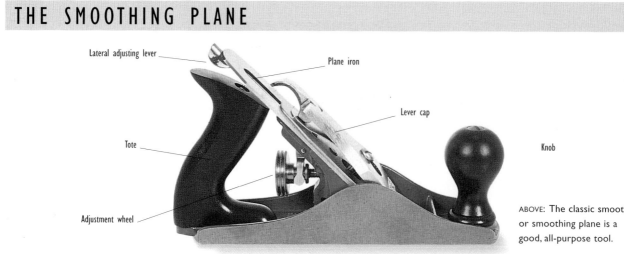

Lateral adjusting lever

Plane iron

Lever cap

Tote

Knob

Adjustment wheel

ABOVE: The classic smooth or smoothing plane is a good, all-purpose tool.

The smoothing or smooth plane has been described variously as a good starter plane, a good all-purpose plane and the plane to buy if you plan to get just one large plane. Although the smooth plane won't finish an edge as well as a jointer plane, and it won't handle end grain as well as a block plane, it is still more versatile than any other single plane. The metal smooth plane has a sole 23–25.5 cm (9–10 in) long and a cutter that is ground square. However, there is some dispute about how precisely a smoothing

ABOVE: Battens and bench stop for holding the wood.

plane iron ought to be ground and honed. Some woodworkers prefer the edge to be straight with the corners sharp and at right angles, while others opt for having the edge straight but the corners slightly rounded. They maintain that the round corners avoid making scratches and ridges in the workpiece. If you are a beginner, the best approach is to start out with the straight edge and then if you run into problems try rounding the corners. The one sure-fire rule about using a smoothing plane is that the lateral lever must be perfectly set so that the cutting edge is parallel to the mouth.

Smoothing Defined

The technique of using a plane to take the surface of a board to a level flat finish, is termed "smoothing". The aim of the operation is to prepare the surface for the final scraping. Most woodworkers would agree that smoothing is a pivotal technique that needs to be mastered. If you can smooth up a surface with a plane, then you can go straight from smoothing through to scraping without the wearisome surface-blurring chore of sanding. Though it has been said that the use of milled lumber negates the need for the smoothing plane, the simple truth is that most so-called "prepared" wood is full of ripples, ridges and scuffs.

Holding the Workpiece

The first thing that you have to figure out before you ever start smoothing is how to hold and secure the wood. Though it will, to a large extent, depend on the size of the board, most woodworkers go for having the

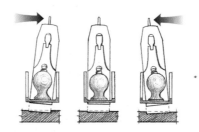

ABOVE: Check blade isn't skewed which would result in an uneven surface.

end butted against one or more bench stops and the sides contained by nailed battens. But no matter how you do it, the board must be completely flat, the stops must be set lower than the surface to be planed, and the board should be arranged so that you are working with the grain.

Using the Plane

Once you have the work properly secured, set the plane's cutter and blade depth for the merest skimming cut and then start work. Test that the shavings are paper thin – this is most important – then start at the far end of the board and skim off the high spots. Work with a skewed, drifting stroke, all the while backing up along the length of the board. When you think that the surface is nearly smooth, set a straight edge across the width and take a sighting to see if light shines through. If

ABOVE: Direction of cut.

you still see light, then repeat the procedure. It's all pretty straightforward, as long as the blade is set for the lightest of lightest cuts. And just in case you think that the need for a fine cut is a lot of blather, some old-time woodworkers finish up with the plane so exquisitely tuned that the final smoothing is more like polishing than cutting.

Smoothing

Certainly power thicknessers are truly wonderful for all manner of tasks, but only the biggest industrial models can handle smoothing wide glued-up panels like table tops. If you want to save money by gluing up narrow sections and then smoothing – rather than buying expensive wide boards – or you simply want to master an age-old technique, then the following project will show you how.

1 Spend time tuning and setting up the plane. Make sure that the cutting edge of the blade is parallel to the mouth.

2 With the workpiece well secured, start at the end farthest away from you and make a series of slightly skewed shearing strokes.

3 Use a square to check that the face and the edge are true and square to each other.

4 If you are after a super smooth finish, and if the length of wood allows, then avoid running the plane off the end of the wood. The best procedure when you come to the end of the stroke is to ease off the pressure on the front knob, so that the plane ceases to cut. In this way, you will avoid rounding the wood over and/or marking the wood with the back end of the plane.

TIPS BOX

Though a modern power planer is great for achieving a quick finish, the design of these machines is such that the blades soon become nicked. When this happens, the resultant boards show thin ridges that run in the direction of the grain. So what to do? The answer is to take out the ridges with a smoothing plane!

THE BLOCK PLANE

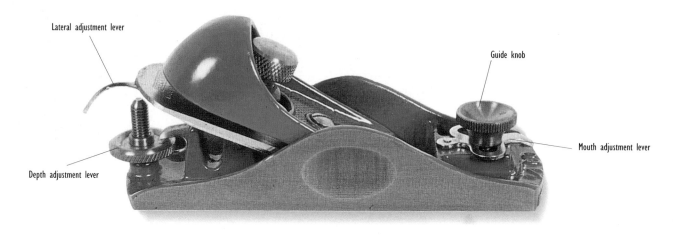

Lateral adjustment lever

Guide knob

Depth adjustment lever

Mouth adjustment lever

ABOVE: Low-angle block plane for use on laminates and end grain.

Designed originally for trimming up the end-grain surface of butcher blocks, block planes are different from the large bench planes in just about every respect. For example, a block plane has a single blade rather than a paired-up cutter and cap iron, and the block plane cutter is reversed so that the bevel is facing up and set at a low angle. The most obvious difference of all is that the block plane at about 14–15.25 cm (5½–6 in) long is small enough to fit into the hand. All this adds up to a precision tool that is designed specifically to plane end grain. Though the beginner might well be confused by the number and type of block planes on the market, the main differences between models has to do with ease of adjustment

ABOVE: Holding the block plane.

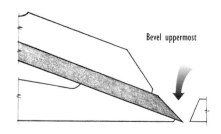

Bevel uppermost

ABOVE: Cross-section showing the bevel and mouth.

rather than function. Certainly a screw adjustment for blade advancement is a good idea, and a lever for lateral control makes it that much easier to set the blade. But the only difference that affects function is the angle of the blade. There are two angles to choose from: the 20-degree angle for general tasks, and the extra-low 12-degree angle for very hard wood or for troublesome grain. If you want to buy a block plane second-hand, then you might well look out for the choice double-ended bullnose block plane, which is now out of production. It is the perfect block plane for general work and for planing into tight corners.

Block Plane Technique

It is impossible for the serious woodworker to get by without the block plane. It is the first-choice tool for all the little tidying tasks. It is most important that you master the following techniques.

Pulling

This is a simple technique in which the user holds the block plane back to front and in both hands, and then pulls the plane rather than pushing it. This is particularly useful when you want to work end grain from side-to-centre, such as when you can't get the plane to push easily from the other side.

Shearing

This technique is perfect for planing tough end-grain wood. The plane is held firmly in one hand so that you can put all the power of your shoulder behind the stroke. Then you run the plane with a sideways sliding or shearing cut. If the cutter is well honed and you catch the grain right, you will achieve a silky smooth surface that won't need sanding.

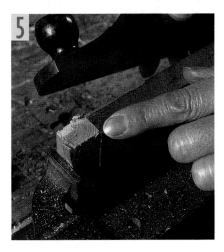

1 Set the workpiece in the vice so that the end grain face is uppermost and clamp strips of waste at both the end and the start of the run. Make sure that the wasters are perfectly aligned with the edges to be planed.

2 Turn the plane over so that you can sight down the length of the sole, then advance the blade and make a trial cut. Repeat this procedure until you achieve the finest cut.

3 If need be, adjust the lateral control.

4 If the plane is correctly tuned, and your technique is good, the resulting surface will be perfectly smooth and almost polished.

5 If the wasters are correctly placed and clamped, they will take any splitting damage rather than the workpiece.

TIPS BOX

There is something special about a well-tuned block plane. Maybe it's the small size, or the fact that it feels like an extension of the arm, or perhaps it's simply that the block plane gets the job done. No matter – suffice it to say that many woodworkers are fascinated by block planes – especially the old, out-of-production types. Many of these old planes are better made and less expensive than new models.

The following out-of-production planes are just a few of the many that are revered by both users and collectors:
• The Record No.0130 bullnose is a choice item – able to cut shavings as thin as .02 mm (.001 in).
• The Record No.0100 1/2 is great for model making, with a sole convex in both width and length.
• The Union No.138 Knuckle-joint lever plane 1905, with an improved throat adjustment.
• The Union No.101, called a toy block plane because of its 7.5-cm (3-in) length.

THE BENCH REBATE PLANE

The first thing to get sorted is the name. Rebate is the ancient term that is dominant in America and some parts of the UK, while rebate is the term that is currently coming into more favour in Britain. A bench rebate plane is designed specifically to cut a step or rebate along the edge of a board. The feature that enables it to do what it does is the open throat, allowing the cutter iron to extend to the outside face or cheeks of the plane body. This feature allows the plane to make a right-angled rebate that is as wide as the sole of the plane. In use, the plane is handled in much the same way as any large bench plane, the only difference being that it is mostly used in conjunction with a wood strip or fence.

ABOVE: The bench rebate plane – with the characteristic open cheeks.

THE REBATE FILISTER PLANE

When a rebate plane is fitted with its own fence, it becomes the rebate filister. With its adjustable fence, depth gauge and side body spurs, this beautiful plane is designed to cut rebates up to 3.8 cm (1½ in) wide and 64 mm (¾ in) deep. The features that make this plane so special are the spurs that enable it to cut across end grain, and the bull nose that allows the blade to be relocated so that it can cut into tight corners. To properly use the rebate filister plane first secure the workpiece in the vice, and adjust the fence to the width of the rebate. The depth guide is positioned

RIGHT: The rebate filister is also called simply a filister. The cutter can be used in the forward position for bullnose work.

Forward position for cutter

Fence adjustment screw

to the desired depth. The plane is then set down on the farthest end of the board, the fence is clenched hard up against the side of the board and the rebate is run. This procedure allows you to gradually back up as the rebate is cut.

THE BULLNOSE PLANE

Bullnose or bullnosed planes are perfect for skimming, trimming and tidying up tasks. With the cutting iron running the full width of the sole – like a rebate plane – and with some planes having a removable nose, they are designed specifically to trim rebates and wide housings. Though there are many types of bullnose planes to choose from, some with many add-ons and embellishments, the main differences between models have to do with ease of adjustment rather than function. As with all low-pitch planes, the blade is always set bevel side up.

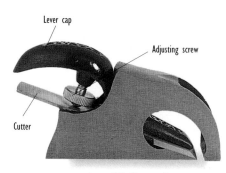

Lever cap

Adjusting screw

Cutter

ABOVE: A small bullnose plane.

RIGHT: Tidying up end grain with a bullnose plain.

THE SHOULDER PLANE

The shoulder plane might almost be described as a small rebate plane since it also has the mouth open at the sides or cheeks and a blade that is the full width of the sole. With the blade set bevel up and at and low angle of about 20 degrees, this plane is designed specifically to clean up end grain shoulders, as well as the end-grain presented in various other fancy cabinet joints.

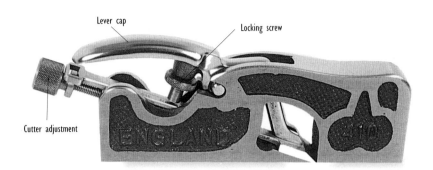

Lever cap

Locking screw

Cutter adjustment

ABOVE: The classic shoulder plane – the perfect tool for shooting shoulders and trimming up dovetails.

THE THREE-IN-ONE SHOULDER PLANE

The 3-in-1, sometimes also called a chisel bullnose, is a beautiful little plane of the shoulder plane type. It is a cross between a shoulder, a bullnose and a chisel plane. With open cheeks – the same as the rebate plane and the bullnose – it is special in that bits and parts can be removed and reset so that it can be used to perform various specific tasks. Certainly, there is no doubt that it takes some fiddling to set up and adjust this plane, with its ingenious interchange of screws and shims. But then again, it does do the work of three planes.

The chisel plane proper is unique in that it has no support in front of the blade. This detail makes it totally useless for general work, but it is a plane that is supremely dedicated to the single task of paring into tight corners. The question you have to ask yourself is do you want a single plane that is pretty good for a range of tasks? If you answer yes, you might go for the 3-in-1. If, however, you want lots of individual planes, each dedicated to a single task, then the 3-in-1 may not be for you.

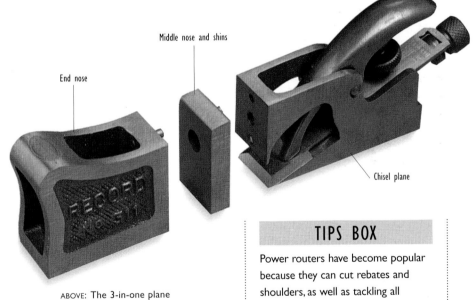

End nose

Middle nose and shins

Chisel plane

ABOVE: The 3-in-one plane is a combined shoulder, bullnose and chisel plane – a fully adjustable tool.

TIPS BOX

Power routers have become popular because they can cut rebates and shoulders, as well as tackling all manner of other tasks with their speed and power. But you have to ask yourself do you want to go down the router road of speed and noise or would you rather take the quiet hand-plane road of take-your-time? That said, there are plenty of woodworkers who claim that a well-tuned plane is as fast or faster than a router, considering the lengthy set-up and adjustment work a router usually requires.

THE PLOUGH PLANE

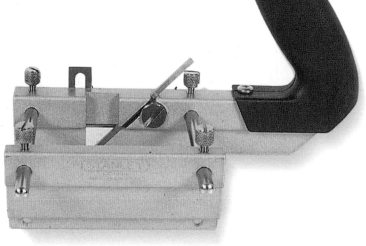

LEFT: The plough plane is designed specifically to cut grooves and channels.

The plough plane – also called a plow plane or a grooving plane – is a plane that is dedicated to cutting grooves and channels. It will also cut small rebates and tongues. To use the plane, first fit it with a blade width to suit, say a 30 mm ($\frac{1}{8}$ in), a 60 mm ($\frac{1}{4}$ in) or whatever, adjust the fence so that the groove is the correct distance in from the edge of the board and adjust the depth gauge to the depth of the groove. Next, clench the plane against the far end edge of the workpiece and then run the cut. The grooving plane is wonderfully easy to use, but only if you obey the three golden rules: always set the blade for the lightest possible cut, always hold the fence hard up against the edge, and always hold the plane upright so that the sides of the groove are at right angles to the face of the workpiece.

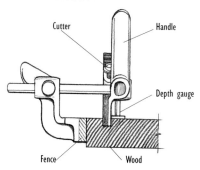

ABOVE: Cross-section showing how the fence and the sole of the plane relate to the wood.

1 Use a ruler to set the spacing between the side of the plane and the fence, then make several trial runs until you are satisfied that all is correct.

2 Hold the fence hard up against the side of the workpiece, making sure that the handle is upright, and be careful not to force the pace. If the plane is correctly tuned, then its weight alone will do most of the work.

TIPS BOX

Thirty or so years ago, there were all manner of exciting fun-to-use, all-metal plough planes on the market. Now there are just a couple. Many woodworkers go for the second-hand option, looking for planes made from the 1940s through to the early 1960s. There are three good reasons to choose an older plane: they are quality tools; they are less expensive than new; and, of course, there is greater choice.

ROUTER PLANES

Coming in various sizes, the router plane is designed specifically to smooth the bottom of channels and grooves, such as stopped housings and recesses for locks and hinges. To use a router plane, first define the width of the channel with saw cuts and set the foot-like cranked cutter to make the shallowest possible cut. Next, make decisions as to whether or not you want to have the mouth open or closed and set the depth gauge. Finally, take the tool in both hands and work with an even, pushing stroke.

1 Adjust the foot blade so that it makes the finest cut and set the depth gauge at the required depth.

2 Hold the tool firmly in both hands and make a series of advancing cuts. Be careful that you don't run off course and do damage to the sides of the trench.

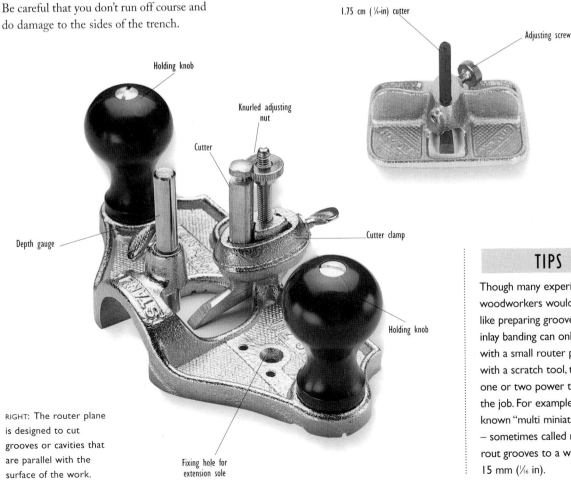

1.75 cm (¼-in) cutter

Adjusting screw

Holding knob

Knurled adjusting nut

Cutter

Depth gauge

Cutter clamp

Holding knob

Fixing hole for extension sole

LEFT: Miniature router for delicate work such as carved work, lettering, veneers and inlays.

RIGHT: The router plane is designed to cut grooves or cavities that are parallel with the surface of the work.

TIPS BOX

Though many experienced hand tool woodworkers would claim that a task like preparing grooves for miniature inlay banding can only be managed with a small router plane or maybe with a scratch tool, there are now one or two power tools that can do the job. For example, some well-known "multi miniature power tools" – sometimes called moto-tools – can rout grooves to a width of less than 15 mm (¹⁄₁₆ in).

THE COMPASS PLANE

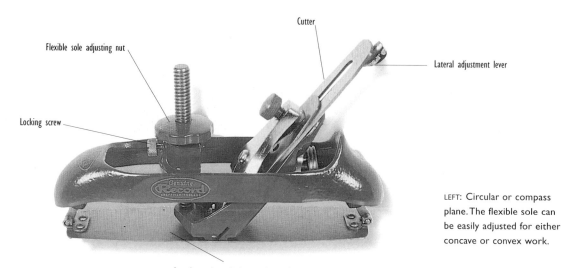

Cutter

Flexible sole adjusting nut

Lateral adjustment lever

Locking screw

One-piece sole made from spring steel

LEFT: Circular or compass plane. The flexible sole can be easily adjusted for either concave or convex work.

The compass plane – also known variously as the circular plane and the wheelwright's plane – is designed to plane concave and convex curves. Traditionally, the compass plane was made of wood, with separate concave and convex planes in a great range of sizes. So, for example, a nineteenth-century furniture maker producing round-top tables or the carpenter making bow windows and curve-top doors would have had whole sets of compass planes – one plane for each circle size. Instead, the modern all-metal compass plane is fitted with a flexible sole that can be adjusted for a whole range of sizes and for both inside and outside curves. You need only one plane. The whole adjustment of the frog, the cutter and the lateral lever is more or less identical to that found on most large bench planes. The cutter can be ground and honed in just the same way as for the bench plane. In fact, the only difference between the modern compass plane and its bench plane buddies is that the sole can be flexed to take on a curved profile.

LEFT: Make adjustments until the curve of the sole is an easy fit on the wood to be worked. Be sure to work in the direction of the grain so that you don't cut directly into the endgrain.

When to Use a Compass Plane

The compass plane is an indispensable tool for woodworkers who want to produce curved work. It's the perfect tool for such projects as round-top tables, curved windowsills, curved cabinet construction, arched door tops, bow-fronted chests and all the other tasks that just can't be done with a flat-soled plane. Of course, you could use a drawknife to shape large convex curves on traditional farmhouse pieces like Windsor chairs and round-top chests that benefit by having "free" curves, but for pieces of formal furniture that are going to be worked with moulding planes or perhaps veneered, there is no choice but to use a compass plane. Don't expect to save money by shopping for an old used compass plane: they are so fascinating and intricate and so altogether attractive to hold, that they have become highly collectable, with old planes costing more than new.

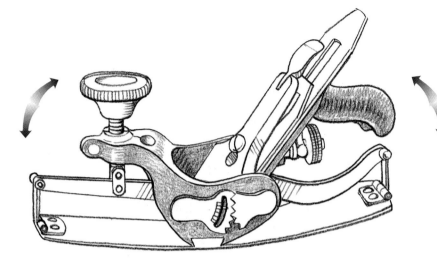

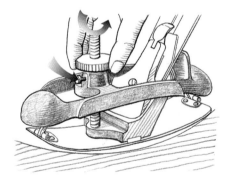

ABOVE: Another type of compass plane. Both ends of the sole move up and down, operated by levers connected to the adjustment screw.

RIGHT: Adjust the sole of the plane in the concave curve of the workpiece, until a slightly loose, rocking fit is achieved.

ABOVE: Adjusting the sole. When completed, tighten the locking screw.

ABOVE: Adjust the sole to a smaller curve than the workpiece when working concave shapes.

Compass Plane Technique

Before using a compass plane, first rough out the profile with a bow saw. Then secure the workpiece curve-side-up in the jaws of the vice. Take the plane and start by winding the cutter back out of harm's way. Set the plane down on or in the curve and adjust the large screw until the sole of the plane achieves a comfortable mating fit on the surface to be worked. When working concave curves, some woodworkers prefer to have the adjustment set slightly acute so that the sole is fractionally tighter than the curve to be worked. That way the plane rocks in the direction of its length. When you are happy with the set of the curve, tighten the locking screw and get ready for action. Check the grain direction, make sure that you are working with the grain, not against it, and then take the cut. Though it's all pretty straightforward, the mistake that most beginners make at this stage is they try to twist or skew the plane – as they might rightly do when using the smoothing plane to make a skewed, shearing cut. But the compass plane has to be run straight-on, no shearing or cross-cut skewing. The only other problem that some beginners run into is that they try to work the whole curve in the same direction. For example, when they are planing the edge of a circular table they might start at the 12 o'clock position and work clockwise around the whole circle. Well, of course, if you look to the grain of a circle, you will see that to keep planing with the grain you have to change direction for each quarter circle.

TIPS BOX

Though the power router is great for all manner of curved work, there is no contest when it comes to wide, glued-up constructions like the fronts of serpentine and bow-fronted chests. In this case, the compass plane is the only tool for the task.

WOODEN MOULDING PLANES

Mouldings are decorative three-dimensional profiles that draw their inspiration from classic architectural forms. For example, the curved profile that runs around the edge of a table, and the fancy architraves that run around doors and windows, the shaped beadings that run around panels and shaped bannister rails are all mouldings that have their roots in classical Greek and Roman forms. Consequently, the moulded shapes mostly have Latin names, like cavetto, ovolo, astragal, cyma reversa, and so on. From ancient times right through to the beginning of the twentieth century, all the mouldings in woodwork were made with wooden planes. With each and every design or profile being worked in a whole range of sizes, it is estimated that the average nineteenth century woodworker might well have had 40–50 different moulding planes. Most moulding planes are out of production and can only be bought second-hand.

Hollows and Rounds

The first thing to understand with hollows and rounds is that the two names describe the shape of the planes, rather than the profiles they produce. So, in fact, a "hollow" plane makes a round convex shape, and a "round" plane cuts a hollow or concave shape. Coming in sets of paired hollows and rounds, the width of the blade at the cutting edge is the same as the radius from which the curve is struck. For example, a 1.75 cm (¹/₂-in)-wide hollow plane will cut a profile belonging to a 2.5 cm (1-in)-diameter circle.

Tongues and Grooves

Certainly tongue-and-groove or match planes are not moulding planes proper – after all, the resultant profile is functional rather than decorative – but in terms of structure and operation they are close relatives of the moulding plane family. They either come in paired sets or there are dual-purpose planes that do both tasks.

Bead Plane

Bead moulding planes are designed to cut a convex bead along the side edge of a board. Since a bead is a very good way of concealing a joint – either at a corner or at a butting together of two boards – these planes were very common. They were sold individually or in sets. The best planes of this type were fitted with boxwood slips to make the delicate parts of the sole stand up to wear. In use, they are run along the edge of a board in much the same way as you would use a rebate plane.

Ogee Plane

The ogee moulding, sometimes called a Grecian or Greek ogee, was a very popular type of decoration in the late eighteenth and early nineteenth century. In form it is much the same as a bead, but the convex and concave profiles run together to make a flat "S" shape. There were many ogee forms. The deep grooves cut by these planes were called "quirks", and the best quality planes have the quirk-cutting part of the sole made from an inset slip of boxwood.

ABOVE: **A matching pair of hollow and round moulding planes.**

ABOVE: **A 2-in-1 tongue and groove moulding plane.**

Roman Ovolo Plane

The Roman ovolo moulding plane – much used in the eighteenth and nineteenth centuries – produced a quarter-circle profile with a small step at top and bottom. Georgian woodworkers were very concerned with scale and proportion, so each size of ovolo plane was designed to be used with a particular thickness of wood.

Panel-raising Plane

Though a panel-raising plane is not strictly a moulding plane, it is very often used in conjunction with moulding planes and, of course, it is much the same in structure. A raised panel is an area in high relief – like a plateau – surrounded by a wide lowered area – like a wide rebate. The panel-raising plane is the tool that is used to create the step. These planes have an adjustable depth stop, a fixed or adjustable fence and a skewed cutting iron. If the plane is designed to cut a sloping step or border, then the sole of the plane is angled.

Boxed Triple Reed

In the middle of the nineteenth century it was very fashionable to have two, three, four or more lines of beaded decoration, especially on wood panel trim and around door frames and windows. Though the moulding planes that were used to cut these convex beads are sometimes called beading planes, they are more commonly called multiple reeding planes – from the shape of the plane sole. The best quality multiple small-size reeding planes have a boxwood sole that is dovetailed into a beech base.

LEFT: Ogee plane – with characteristic flat "s" profile and inset "quirk" slip.

RIGHT: Triple-reed – a good quality plane with a fully-boxed sole.

LEFT: Beading plane – designed to cut a bead profile on the edge of a board.

RIGHT: Roman Ovolo plane.

LEFT: Panel-raising plane – with a skewed blade and an adjustable fence.

COMBINATION AND MULTI-PLANES

Toward the end of the nineteenth century, there was a huge push to develop multi-purpose iron planes. Remember, that at that time, the skilled woodworker had to have all manner of dedicated single-task wooden planes – a set of grooving planes, a set of hollows and rounds, and so on – for all the many grooving and shaping tasks.

Manufacturers came up with the brilliant idea of making one plane that could do it all. Through an evolutionary process they developed several do-it-all planes that came to be known variously as universal combination planes and multi-planes. With the primary manufacturer being "Stanley" in America, and then later "Record" in England, the best planes of this type are the "Stanley 45", the "Record 405", which was a copy of the "Stanley", and the legendary "Stanley 55". These planes are characterized by having a main stock with a handle, a cutter clamp and depth gauge, two bar arms that are fixed to the stock with screws, a middle section with an integral handle and runner that slides onto the arms, and then a fence and/or another handle that also slides onto the arms.

To use one of these planes, one of the many cutters is selected and fitted, the middle sliding section is brought up close to the cutter and then the fence and depth stops are adjusted to suit. The cutter is set for a shallow cut, and then the plane is used in much the same way as a rebate plane. Certainly it sounds a bit whiz-bang, but in fact it is a very exciting and successful tool. Though the "Stanley" and "Record" planes are long out of production, they can be bought used and a manufacturer has started making "Stanley" look-alikes.

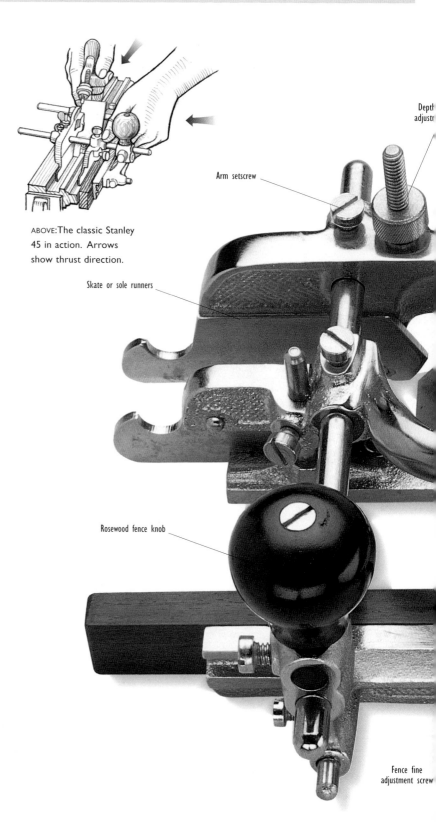

ABOVE: The classic Stanley 45 in action. Arrows show thrust direction.

Depth adjustr

Arm setscrew

Skate or sole runners

Rosewood fence knob

Fence fine adjustment screw

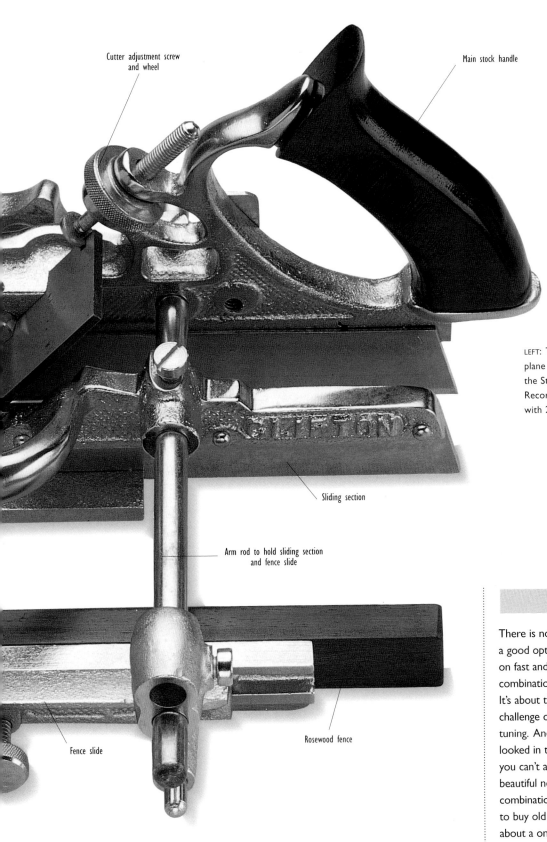

Cutter adjustment screw
and wheel

Main stock handle

Sliding section

Arm rod to hold sliding section
and fence slide

Fence slide

Rosewood fence

LEFT: The Clifton multi-plane is the successor to the Stanley 45 and the Record 405 – it is supplied with 24 cutters.

TIPS BOX

There is no denying that the router is a good option if your income depends on fast and furious output. But a combination plane isn't about speed. It's about the simple pleasure and challenge of all the setting up and tuning. And just in case you have looked in the catalogue and see that you can't afford the high price of the beautiful new reproduction combination planes, it is still possible to buy old models second-hand at about a one third the cost of new.

USING THE "STANLEY 45" COMBINATION PLANE

Using a combination plane is great fun and altogether wonderful, but only if it is perfectly set up and finely tuned. The following pointers will help you on your way.

The Cutters

The cutters must be razor sharp. They need to be ground to a 35-degree primary bevel and then honed to a slightly larger secondary bevel. This is easy enough for the square-end cutters: All you do is grind them square and then hone them on a flat stone. The shaped cutters are best honed with little slipstones in much the same way as when sharpening gouges and knives. Don't forget to remove the burr with a slip or strop.

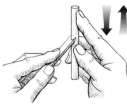

ABOVE: Sharpening the cutters.

The Depth of Cut

The depth of cut must always be set for the finest of fine cuts. The best procedure is to wind the cutter back out of the way and then advance little by little until you are producing a tissue-fine shaving. If you find the going difficult, then either the cutting edge is less than perfect or your wood is knotty, ragged, damp or all of these.

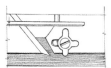

ABOVE: The spur is set so that it prepares the way for the cut.

RIGHT: Cross-section view of the bead cutter.

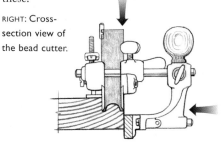

Setting the Spurs

The spurs are designed specifically to cut the fibres of the wood when you are working across the grain. The idea is that the spurs score the wood and prepare the way for the cutters. The best procedure is to start the cut with a dragging stroke at the farthest end of the board. You will find that the dragging lets the spurs do their stuff. Don't forget that the spurs need to be honed from time to time.

Setting the Fence

The metal fence is drilled with a couple of holes so the purchaser can fit a hardwood strip to protect the workpiece from the metal face of the fence and to ease the going. It's best to start all planing operations by burnishing the fence and the soles of the skates with a white candle. You will find that the waxing cuts the amount of effort by half.

Stance and Starting

After adjusting the plane, waxing the sole and fence and selecting a straight-grained wood, then spend time making sure that the wood is well secured in the vice and/or with clamps. Make sure you can take a clear run from one end of the wood through to the other without the body of the plane and/or the fence being obstructed. The best arrangement is to have the wood to be worked with its edge hanging out over the side of the bench, so that there is plenty of room for the hand that is holding and supporting the fence. When you are ready to start, hold the body of the plane upright, check that the fence is hard up against the edge and then make the first cut. The key pointers to success are: let the weight of the plane do the work, and make sure all along the way that the fence is hard up against the edge of the workpiece.

1 Check that the component parts are in good order.

2 Set your choosen cutter blade in place and make sure that it is notched onto the adjustment wheel.

3 Slide the second skate-sole in place and carefully align it with the side of the cutter blade.

4 Slide the fence in place and use a ruler to set the spacing.

5 Start at the end of the wood farthest away from you and take the first cut. Make sure that you use your left hand to hold the fence hard up against the workpiece.

6 Once you have repeatedly backed-and-advanced to the full length of the workpiece, then make a series of through-cuts to clean out the profile.

7 If you have done it right, then the beading should look crisp and clean and almost polished.

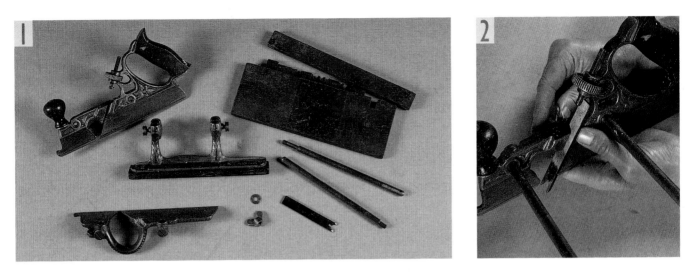

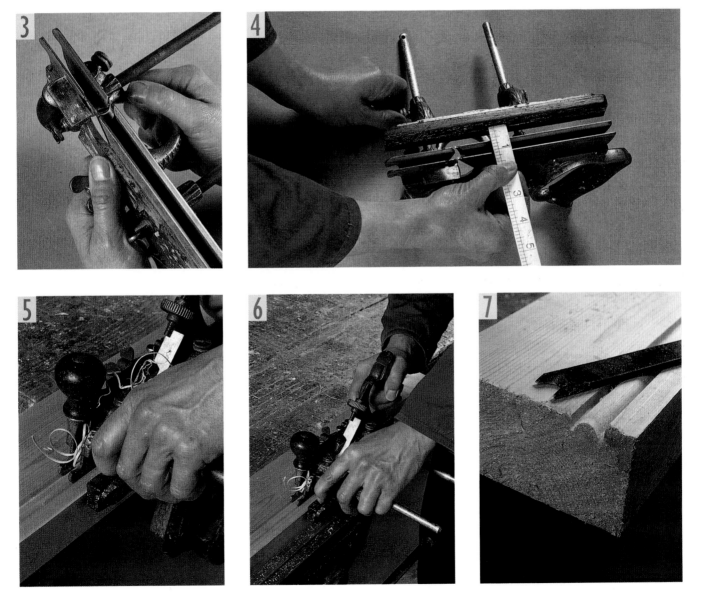

Drilling

The woodworker is forever needing to make holes in wood for screws, dowels, nails, bolts and for many other reasons besides. The traditional hand brace has, to some extent, been dropped in favour of the portable power drill, and certainly the electric drill press is good for boring large diameter holes. But that said, just about every other hole-boring operation that you can think of can be performed with more accuracy, sensitivity and speed with one of the hand drill options. If you want to achieve maximum control with minimum effort, then you need to get yourself one or two inexpensive hand drills and bone up on a few easily learned techniques.

THE BRACE

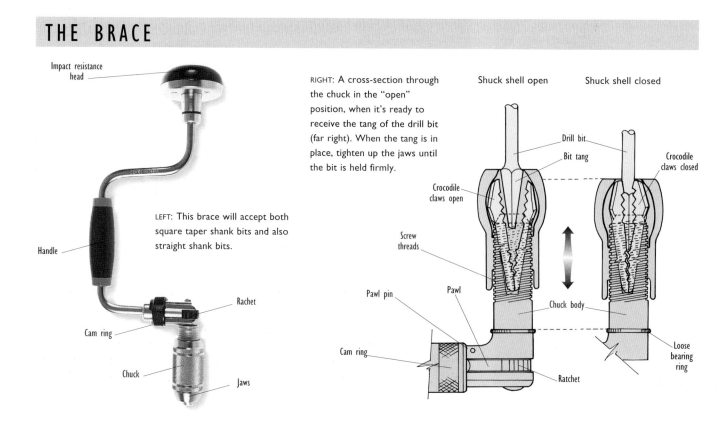

Impact resistance head

Handle

Cam ring

Chuck

Rachet

Jaws

LEFT: This brace will accept both square taper shank bits and also straight shank bits.

RIGHT: A cross-section through the chuck in the "open" position, when it's ready to receive the tang of the drill bit (far right). When the tang is in place, tighten up the jaws until the bit is held firmly.

Shuck shell open

Shuck shell closed

Drill bit

Bit tang

Crocodile claws open

Crocodile claws closed

Screw threads

Pawl pin

Pawl

Cam ring

Ratchet

Chuck body

Loose bearing ring

The woodworker's brace has, in various guises, been around for about 400 years. Used to bore holes in wood, the brace is a wonderfully efficient tool that is just about as foolproof as a tool can get. In form, it is a crank-shaped tool that has a pad or head on one end, a handle at the middle of the crank and a chuck with a set of bit-gripping jaws on the business end.

The working action is beautifully simple: the brace applies a turning force to the drill bit, by means of a crank or frame.

The Sweep

The distance between the centre of spin and the crank handle is termed the "half sweep" or the "throw" or the "half-swing" and is like the radius of a circle. The

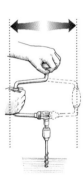

bigger the total sweep, the more efficient the drilling action. For efficiency, the rule is: the bigger the hole to be drilled or bored, then the bigger the sweep size. Braces are sometimes sold according to the size of the throw or swing and sometimes according to the total diameter size. Either way – it doesn't matter too much – all you have to know is the bigger the crank, then the easier it is to turn the drill bit.

ABOVE: The sweep of the brace.

The Cam Ring and Ratchet

The cam ring and ratchet is a clever little mechanism that allows the user to change the direction of the action. There are three settings: cam clockwise and against the stop for positive drilling; cam at the centre for drilling in either direction; and cam

RIGHT: The cam ring action.

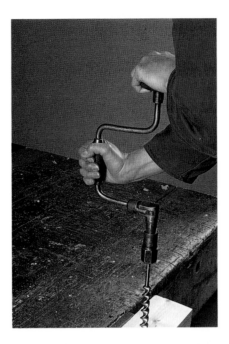

against the left stop for withdrawing the drill bit. The ratchet allows the user to repeatedly swing the drill forwards a partial turn, then back up and repeat so that a hole can be drilled without swinging the handle through a whole circle. This is particularly useful in difficult-to-work areas when you can't get to swing the crank in a full circle, like the corner of a frame.

The Chuck and Jaws

Most traditional braces are fitted with "V" crocodile jaws that are designed to grip tapered, square-tanged bits. To install a bit, set the cam in the middle position, open the chuck jaws good and wide, pop the tang of the drill bit in the jaws, check that the bit is square with the crank and then tighten up.

To Drill Vertically

First use an awl, bradawl or small drill to establish the centre point in the workpiece. To start drilling, turn the ratchet clockwise to the stop pin, set the bit in the pilot hole, apply pressure to the head of the brace, making sure that the brace is square and well aligned. Then turn the crank in a clockwise direction until the hole is drilled to depth. To withdraw the bit, simply turn the cam ring to the anti-clockwise position and turn the crank in the anti-clockwise direction.

To Drill Horizontally

After making the pilot hole and setting the cam ring as already described, set the bit in the hole. Hold and support the brace head with your hand and body, and then simultaneously put your weight against the brace, while checking alignment and turning.

LEFT: To tighten up, hold the chuck and turn the brace.

AUGER TWIST BITS

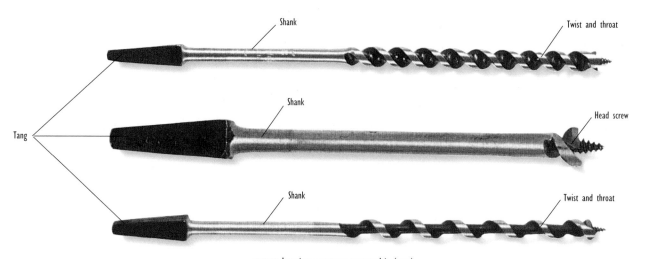

ABOVE: Jennings pattern screw bit (top),
Centre pattern screw bit (middle) and Solid-centre bit
(bottom) can all be used in a traditional brace.

Known variously as an auger screw bit, an auger twist bit, a twist auger bit, a spiral auger bit and one or two other names besides, the auger bit is a really good option for boring deep holes. The lead screw drags the body of the bit into the wood. However, finding the right one can be confusing.

The following pointers and definitions will help you to understand your needs and keep your auger bits in good order.

Lead Screw

The screw point at the business end of the auger bit is termed the "lead screw" or the "screw lead". There are three grades of lead screw, slow, medium and fast. The function of the lead screw is to seat into the pilot hole, to get a bite into the wood, and then to drag the body of the bit through the wood at a regulated speed. The faster the lead screw, the faster the speed of the bit through the wood, and consequently the coarser the cut. You have to decide whether you want a fast, ragged hole or a slow, fine one.

Cutting Spurs

Once the lead screw starts to drag the bit into the wood, the next part of the head to come into contact is the cutting spur or fluke. Auger bit types have all manner of spur configurations, but the function of the spur remains the same: to define and score the circumference of the hole.

ABOVE:: The lead screw drags the body of the bit into the wood.

Cutting Lips

Once the spur has defined the hole by scoring the circumference, the cutting lips come into contact with the wood and slice out a layer of waste.

Twist and Throat

The twist and throat work in conjunction with each other to gather up the waste as sliced out by the cutting lips, and direct it up out of the hole.

Shank and Tang

The shank is the length of metal between the upper end of the twist and the beginning of the tang, and the tang is the tapered, square-sectioned end of the bit that fits in the jaws of the brace chuck.

BELOW: The cutting lips slice out layers of waste.

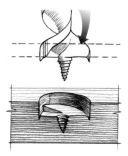

Maintaining and Sharpening a Twist Auger Bit

The twist auger bit is easy to use, lasts a lifetime and is altogether great for boring deep holes, but only if it has been well maintained and sharpened. Just like any other cutting tool, the twist auger bit needs to be kept in good order. It's no good dropping your bits all jumbled in a box and

allowing them to become rusty and dull-edged and then expecting them to do a good job – they won't! Let's say you have inherited some auger bits and they need some reconditioning. The following pointers will allow you to sort out the problems.

ABOVE: Using a bit file edge to sharpen an auger's spurs. Make sure the safe edge of the file is against the lips.

Polishing

The auger needs to be bright and shiny. It might be sharp, but if the whole thing is rusty or has a dull finish, then it's not going to work efficiently. Start by wiping it with spirit and then use the finest wire wool to remove the

ABOVE: Using a bit file to sharpen an auger's lips.

rust. This done, use a buffing wheel or a cloth and polish the whole thing to a bright, shiny finish.

Cleaning the Lead Screw

Remember that the function of the auger

depends on the lead screw dragging the head of the bit into the wood. It's important to make sure that screw grooves are clean and sharp. Take a special bit file or a feather-edge file and work

ABOVE: Hone the cutting lips but be careful not to damage the spurs.

around the screw lead, sharpening up the thread. Don't overdo this stage, just make sure that the threads are clean and defined.

Filing the Spurs and Cutting Lip

With the auger secured head-up in the jaws of a padded vice, take your small file – best if it's a special auger file – and file the inside-edge faces of the spur or spurs. Be careful, because an auger bit without spurs is totally useless. Just settle for a sharp edge. When you repeat the procedure for the cutting lip, work in much the same way as for the spurs, only this time support the bit head-down and file up through the twist or throat so that the bevel is on the underside of the cutting lip.

Honing

After you have cleaned and filed the auger, take a small flat slipstone and spend time honing the cutting bevels of the spurs and the lip to remove the burrs. Finally, wipe the whole thing over with a wax candle and use a cloth to burnish to a high-shine finish.

Using a Twist Auger to Bore a Deep Straight Hole

1 Set the workpiece in the vice so that the hole to be drilled is at a comfortable height and make a few turns until the screw point begins to bite.

2 Check the alignment by eye and then ask a helper to check your approach with a square.

3 Use a ruler and/or a marked dowel to check the depth of the hole.

TIPS BOX

If you enjoy using both power tools and hand tools, then there is an auger bit known as a "combination auger". Designed to be used in power drills and the hand brace, these bits give a deep, crisp-cut hole, with the generous twists or webs resulting in a speedy removal of the waste.

TWIST DRILLS

Handle

Gear wheel

STANLEY
03-105
ENGLAND

Crank drive handle

Drive shaft

Chuck

ABOVE: Single pinion hand drill with die-cast gear wheel.

There are three basic twist drill types: the wheel brace, the breast drill and the archimedean drill. The following listing will help you choose the right drill to meet your needs.

Wheel Brace

The wheel brace, also known as the hand drill and the single-pinion drill, is perhaps the most familiar of all the drill types – the one that gets to be most used and abused. It is sometimes called an "egg-beater drill" because of its resemblance to the common kitchen tool. In form, it usually has two wooden handles, a single pinion, a large open geared wheel and a three-jaw hand-tight chuck. This is the perfect tool for small holes up to about 80 mm (5/16 in). To install the bit, the chuck is opened by hand, the bit is dropped into the three jaws, and the chuck is tightened up. Then the drill is held and supported with one hand, while the geared wheel is turned with the other. The best advice is to let the drill do the work – don't try to apply too much pressure or force the pace.

ABOVE:
Putting the bit in the chuck.

Breast Drill

The breast drill is a large version of the twist drill. It has the same overall shape and structure as the twist drill, but it has a saddle-shaped breast plate, a much larger chuck and a large gear wheel with two gear options. All this adds up to a drill that can be used to bore much larger holes. It is held and

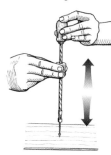

LEFT: Archimedean drill in action.

Swivel handle and bit storage

Drive handle

Screw chuck

ABOVE: Archimedean drill, also called a fret drill, is used for boring small-diameter holes in thin-section wood.

steadied with one hand, while the drive handle is turned with the other. You lean on the breast plate to apply more pressure.

Archimedean Drill

The archimedean drill, also called the fret drill, is the perfect drill for boring small holes in thin wood. In fact it is, as the name suggests, designed to be used in conjunction with a fret saw, making 16 mm (1/16-in)-diameter holes through which the fretsaw blades are threaded. The top handle of the drill is held and supported in one hand, while the lower handle is pumped up and down with the other. If you have in mind to make musical instruments, fine fretwork or small toys, then this is the tool for the job.

USING THE ARCHIMEDEAN DRILL

1 After transferring the design to the wood, then use the archimedean drill to run a small pilot hole through the area of waste. Hold the drill upright and work with an easy constant stroke.

2 Pass the end of the fret saw blade through the pilot hole and hitch up. Make sure that the teeth are pointing down toward the handle.

3 You need to use both hands, one holding and positioning the workpiece so that the blade is presented with the line of the next cut, and the other hand operating the saw.

MAKING AND USING A DEPTH STOP

1 Take your depth stop block – marked 1.25 cm (½ in) – and set the drill bit down in the chuck so that a 1.25 cm (½ in) length of bit sticks out from the end of the block.

2 In use, the block will ensure that the hole runs no deeper than 1.25 cm (½ in).

TWIST BITS

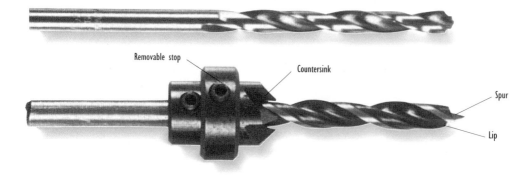

Removable stop   Countersink

Spur

Lip

TOP: Twist drill bit.
BELOW: Combined lip
and spur drill bit with
countersink – good for
countersinking and
boring at the same time.

For working with wood, there are basically two twist drill bit types. There is the twist bit proper – sometimes called a morse drill – that can be used on wood or metal, and there is the brad point bit that is designed specifically to be used with wood.

Twist Drill Bits

Though the twist drill bit was originally developed to drill deep holes in metal, it has gradually come to be accepted as the most suitable bit for boring small holes in wood. With its cylindrical shank, it is designed to be used in the small twist drill. There are several twist bit sub-species, such as for example: blacksmiths bits, long twist bits, and bullet twist bits, but most are not useful for woodworking. Twist bits are fine up to about 96 mm ($^3/_8$ in) or maybe 1.25 cm ($^1/_2$ in), but larger holes are best worked with auger bits.

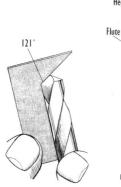

121°

Heel   Chisel edge

Flute   Margin

LEFT: Checking the
angle against a card
template.

1

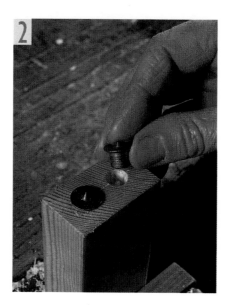

2

3

Brad Point Bits

The brad point bit, sometimes also called the dowel bit or lip and spur bit, was developed to be used with wood. While many consider that the twist bit does an adequate job of boring small holes in wood, they all agree that the brad point bit is best for boring precise, well-placed holes. The brad point's two side spurs and centre point, makes it perfect for boring holes through even the toughest wood.

Fitting Dowels

1 Establish the position of the two dowel holes and bore them out with the brad point bit.

2 Push-fit the brass dowel studs in the drilled holes.

3 Set the mating member in place on the dowel-studs, then tap the assembly with a mallet to press-transfer the position of the two dowels.

4 Having drilled out the mating member, glue-fix the two dowels.

5 Smear glue on mating faces and tap the assembly together.

Sharpening Brad Point Bits

The big mistake that many woodworkers make is that they use and abuse twist drill bits and then trash them. This may be satisfactory for inexpensive twist bits, but for good quality brad point bits it makes better sense to resharpen them.

Let's say then that you have a 1.25 cm (¹/₂ in) diameter brad point bit that needs sharpening. Start by making sure that it is straight. There is no saving a bent bit, so check it against a square. Wipe it over with a spirit-soaked cloth and remove all build-up of resin. Secure the bit head-side-up in the jaws of a padded vice, and use a small file or a small cylindrical slipstone to hone the inside flutes, working the hollow between the central spur or brad and the inside face of the outer spur. If you don't have the correct size file or slipstone, then you can get by with a sliver of wood wrapped with a piece of fine-grade emery paper.

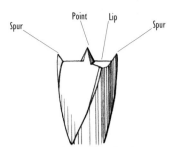

ABOVE A lipped brad point.

ABOVE: Honing a lipped brad point.

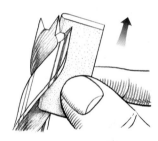

ABOVE: Using a slip stone on a lipped brad-point.

TIPS BOX

Though it is recommended that you use twist drill bits for holes up to 96 mm (⅜ in) diameter, and then use the brace and auger bits for large-diameter holes, if you enjoy using power options like the drill press, you could use large-size spur bits for deep holes up to about 2.5 cm (1 in) diameter, Forstner bits for shallow holes up to about 7.5 cm (3 in) in diameter and flat bits for deep holes where the finish need not be perfectly smooth.

THE EXPANDING BIT

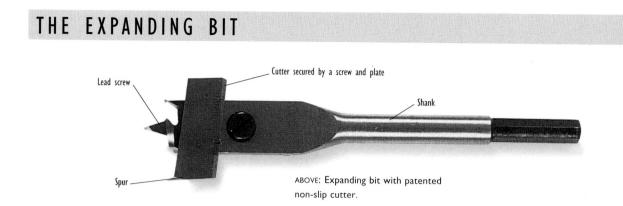

Lead screw

Cutter secured by a screw and plate

Shank

Spur

ABOVE: Expanding bit with patented non-slip cutter.

Known also as an adjusting bit and an expansion bit, the expanding bit is a great tool for woodworkers who need to bore out holes that are larger than those made by the biggest 3.75-cm (1½-in)-diameter auger bit. It allows you to bore an infinite variety of holes up to about 10 cm (4 in) in diameter. It is similar to a centre bit, but it has an adjustable spur cutter. To set up the bit, the side screw is slackened off, the spur cutter is set to the calibrated diameter and then the screw is tightened up.

If you look closely at the expanding bit in action, you will see that the lead screw drags the bit into the wood, the side spur scribes and defines the circumference of the hole, and then the lip cutter sweeps around from the centre point and pares up the waste. When using an expanding bit, you have to maximize your muscle power by using a brace with the biggest possible swing, and you have to make sure that the cutting spurs and lips are razor sharp.

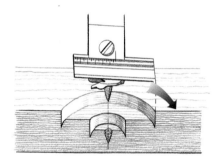

ABOVE Cross-section showing the expansion bit in action.

REAMERS, RIMMERS, RINDERS AND HOLLOW-TAPER BITS

Flute

ABOVE: Step drill – designed to drill and deburr at the same time.

ABOVE: Conical drill

Reamer, rimmer, rinder and hollow-taper bits are all used with a brace or at least alongside a brace to clean out, deburr, enlarge or reshape a hole that has already been bored. In many ways, a reamer might best be considered as a long-nosed countersink. The various types are each designed for a specific task. For example, in guitar and violin making when you need small tapered holes for friction pegs, and in Windsor chair making when you need tapered holes for the chair legs, the best approach is to search out reamer types to meet your needs.

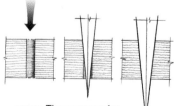

ABOVE: The sequence for reaming a hole.

COUNTERSINKS

RIGHT: Three rose countersinks in various sizes and designs.

Cone shaped cutting end

A countersink is a tool much like a reamer that is designed to cut a bevelled or conical recess. There are two basic types: the hand-held countersink that is used with a quick rotating or reciprocating action and the countersink bit that is used in a brace. Of the drill bit types, there is the conical rosehead and the much older flat V-head. As a general rule, the greater the number of cutting edges and the faster the action, the smoother the resultant countersink.

ABOVE: Give the hand countersink several quick swivel-turns.

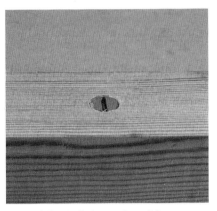

ABOVE: If all is well, the top face of the screw will be a clean fit, but fractionally lower than the surface of the wood.

SPOON BITS

The spoon bit is gouge shaped along its length and enclosed like a spoon at the leading end. It is one of the oldest of all the drill bit types. There are special spoon bits for traditional uses, such as the brushmaker's spoon bit, chairmaker's spoon bit and cooper's spoon bit. Other names describe the form, for example the duck-bill spoon bit and shell spoon bit. The spoon bit is unusual in that the cutting edge isn't dragged into the wood – as with the auger bit – but rather it is simply the downwards pressure that produces the cut. This action makes the spoon bit

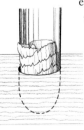

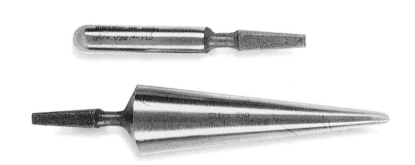

particularly suitable for woodworkers who need simultaneously to drill holes at a low angle and to be in total control of the rate of cut on entry and exit – like Windsor chairmakers.

ABOVE: The spoon bit wins over most other bits in that it can be used either vertically or at an angle.

Sanding and Scraping

Sanding is the procedure of using a variety of sandpapers, rasps and scrapers to produce a finish. Certainly, for many woodworkers, the primary technique relates to using abrasive papers and hand scrapers to create a super-smooth surface, but there are all manner of traditional abrading techniques that have to do with such exciting and dynamic areas of woodworking as sculpting, shaping, texturing and grain enhancement.

ABRASIVE PAPERS

ABOVE: A selection of abrasive papers.

Velcro backed abrasives

Cork

Hard foam

Dual foam block — the soft side is for curved surfaces

ABOVE: Hand sanding blocks.

Sanding

Sanding is the technique of using various abrasives to cut back wood fibres to achieve a smooth finish. As with all the other cutting tools, it is the shape and character of the cutting edge that decides the speed, quality and character of the cut. With abrasives, the cutting edge, or you might more rightly say the cutting teeth, are the crystals that go to make the abrasive. Abrasive papers are sold according to their grit size – the smaller the size, the finer the cut. The following listing will help you match your needs.

ABOVE: The powered anti-dust respirator.

Sandpapers

The term "sandpaper" originally was used to describe an abrasive sheet made up of crushed sand glued to a paper or cloth backing. The term now has come to describe all abrasive papers.

ABOVE: Using the tear-drop sander.

Garnet Paper

Unlike many of the other abrasives, garnet is used specifically for wood. Garnet paper cuts fast, lasts long and achieves a fine soft finish without burning or staining. It's particularly good for resinous wood.

Aluminium Oxide Paper

Aluminium or aluminous oxide is harder and lasts longer than garnet. Known sometimes as aluminium oxide cabinet paper, the name rightly suggests that it is favoured by woodworkers who are

LEFT: Disc sander (lathe attachment).

ABOVE: The traditional quartered-and-torn method of folding abrasive paper ensures that the grit surfaces never meet face to face.

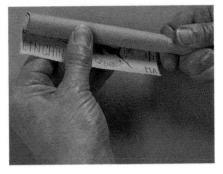

ABOVE: Dowels make good sanding sticks – perfect for cleaning out concave curves.

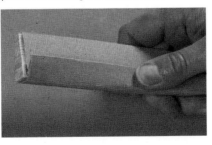

ABOVE: If you need to clean out a narrow slit, a good technique is to wrap the sandpaper around a strip of plywood.

ABOVE: Old timers often made comfortable sanding blocks from scraps of exotic hardwood.

ABOVE: A clever little block device, made in the 1950s, that holds a sheet of sandpaper.

seeking to achieve a soft high-shine finish. Aluminium oxide gives a lighter cut than garnet.

Silicon Carbide Paper

Though silicon carbide or silac carborundum is almost as hard as diamond, woodworkers claim it breaks down more readily than garnet paper. Its use is limited to polishing super-hard woods or in finishing applications.

Steel Wool

Though steel wool is good for cleaning and dulling down painted and glossy finishes, it can stain wood. For example, if you leave the merest particle of steel wool on a piece of damp oak you will be left with a difficult-to-remove black stain. If you intend using steel wool – if only for cleaning your tools – then best go for stainless-steel wool.

Pumice and Rottenstone Powders

Pumice and rottenstone powders are primarily used for cutting down and distressing wood surfaces that have already been finished. For example, if you want to achieve a much-handled-and-worn effect with a piece that has been painted, you could mix the stone powder with a small amount of spirit or wax until you have a paste and then use this as a super-fine rubbing compound. Pumice powder is the first choice for cutting down French polish.

SURFORMS

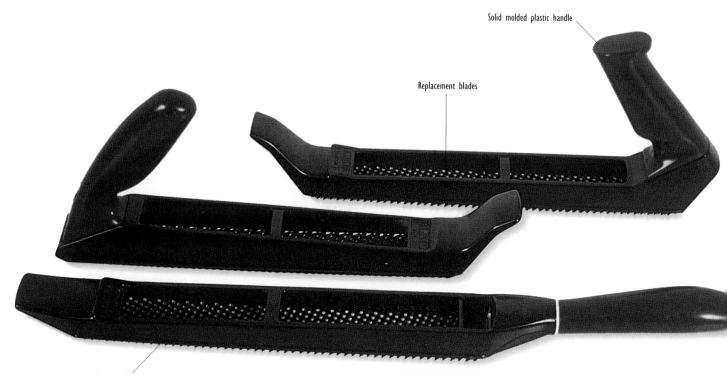

Solid molded plastic handle

Replacement blades

Die-cast alloy body

ABOVE: Standard file (top), planer file (middle) and flat file (bottom).

Surform tools have replaced the more traditional rasps and files for some woodworkers. In form they appear to be a combination of files and planes. Though the open-toothed structure of the surform allows the user to easily cut and shape the wood without worrying about the teeth clogging, this means that the surform needs to be used with care and caution.

LEFT: Though the tube surform is a great tool for cleaning out curve-side pierced holes, you do have to be careful not to run directly into end grain.

TIPS BOX

If you enjoy using power tools, then the power file – a cross between a power drill and a belt sander – is maybe the tool for you. With a finger-like extension that holds and supports a sanding belt at about 1.75 cm (½ in) wide, it is useful for sculpting free-form shapes.

BELOW: Hold the surform with both hands.

RASPS

The rasp is best thought of as the big brother to the file. Files and rasps look much the same – they are both bars of steel of various shapes, lengths and cross-sections, with patterns of teeth cut into their surface. But the file will cut both metal and wood, while the rasp is dedicated to cutting wood. The rasp is held in both hands – one hand gripping the wooden handle and the other hand holding the point at the far end – and then it is variously drawn, stroked, twisted or skew-planed across the workpiece. As with the other cutting tools, best results are achieved when the stroke is made either with or at a slight angle to the grain. Rasps are particularly useful in woodcarving.

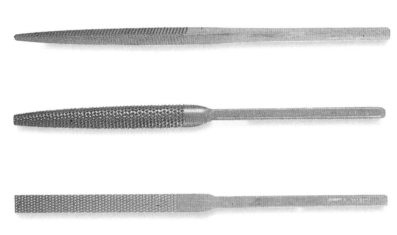

ABOVE: Three carver's rasps – each forged from one piece to create an integral handle.

RIFFLERS

Rifflers are small double-ended rasps. At about 17.75–20.25cm (7–8 in) long, with both ends being the same shape, section and cut, they are perfect for woodcarving. The hooked and pointed shape of the end allows you to work in small, tight, otherwise inaccessible areas. They are particularly useful in relief woodcarving for cutting the lowered ground down to a uniform texture.

They are held at the middle, with the index finger running down the length of the blade, and then used in much the same way as you might use the back of a spoon for burnishing. By using the different shaped rifflers – round, oval, square, triangular, and knife-edge – and by judiciously varying the direction of the stroke, it is possible to achieve a whole range of textural effects. However, you do have to be careful not to overuse rifflers, potentially blurring the sharp corners of the imagery.

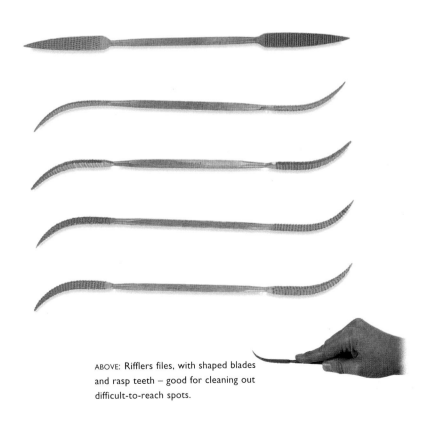

ABOVE: Rifflers files, with shaped blades and rasp teeth – good for cleaning out difficult-to-reach spots.

SCRATCHSTOCK

Adjustable stop or fence

Cutters

ABOVE: A modern German scratchstock – designed for cutting grooves for inlays and beadings.

The first thing you have to understand here is that the term "stock" doesn't refer to the workpiece, but rather it is the older term that describes the piece of shaped wood that goes to make the tool. The scratchstock, sometimes also called variously a scratch tool and a scratch gauge, is usually a homemade tool used for shaping small-section beadings, profiles and grooves. It consists of two identical L-shaped pieces of wood that are screwed together to sandwich and contain a steel cutter. The cutter is filed and ground to the reverse section of the desired moulding or groove. Many woodworkers make scratch stocks from old marking gauges. To use the tool, the wooden stock is butted hard up against the workpiece and then run backwards and forwards with a scraping action. It's perfect for cutting grooves for inlay banding and for shaping short lengths of small-section mouldings.

TIPS BOX

Since the scratchstock is a homemade tool that you shape to suit a particular one-off need, such as making a few inches of non-standard moulding to be used to restore a piece of antique furniture, the power router option is not applicable. However, the best way to shape the scratchstock blades is to use a motor rotary tool fitted with a ruby or diamond bit.

1 After modifying an old marking gauge, and cutting and shaping a piece of spring steel to fit, set the blade in place in the slot, and secure it with a through screw.

2 Drag the scratch stock along the edge of the workpiece so that the blade scratches a reverse profile.

BEADING TOOL

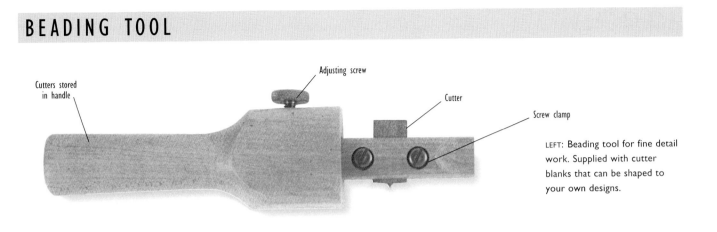

Cutters stored in handle

Adjusting screw

Cutter

Screw clamp

LEFT: Beading tool for fine detail work. Supplied with cutter blanks that can be shaped to your own designs.

The beading tool is a sort of cross between a marking gauge and a scratchstock. There is a central post, a head or fence that slides along the post and a selection of profile cutters that can be fitted to the post. To use the tool, first select a cutter and clamp it in the centre post at roughly the distance to be worked. Set the fence to the correct position and then butt it hard up against the edge of the workpiece. Push and drag the tool alternately backwards and forwards across the workpiece.

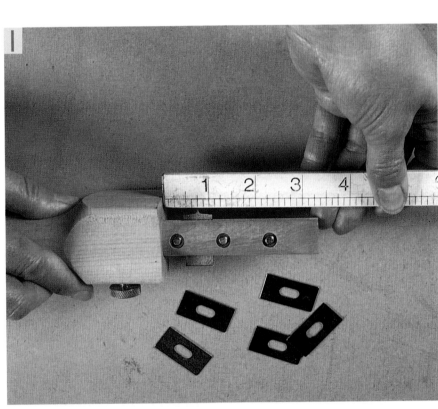

1 Fit the desired cutter blade, making sure that it is perfectly aligned and at the correct depth, then measure, set the fence and tighten up.

2 Set the tool down on the workpiece, adjusting the dragging angle until the blade begins to bite, then make successive passess until the blade ceases to cut.

3 If all is correct, the resulting profile will be clean and burnished.

ABOVE: Hold the beading tool with both hands.

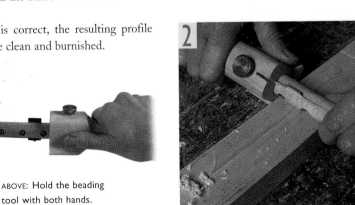

SCRAPERS

All-round cutting edge

ABOVE: Scraper for shaped work.

ABOVE: Scrapers are very useful for removing patches of rough grain in an otherwise smooth surface.

Made from spring steel – like saw blades – scrapers are used for cleaning up the surface of wood prior to the final finishing. There are two basic forms: the rectangular type at about 15 cm (6 in) long and 7.5 cm (3 in) wide, which is used for finishing flat surfaces; and a gooseneck or kidney shape, which comes in various sizes and is used for finishing concave hollows. The scraper is held in both hands, flexed slightly with the thumbs and then either pushed or dragged with the grain, sometimes at a skewed angle. Scrapers are much favoured by cabinetmakers and carvers who are looking to achieve a smooth finish without going to the chore of using sandpaper.

ABOVE: Use a flat file to bring the edge of the scraper to a level clean-cut finish. Repeat this procedure for both cutting edges.

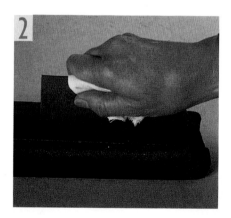

ABOVE: Hold the scraper with a piece of cloth so that you don't cut your hands. Hone the filed edge on a medium stone. Aim for a square-cut polished edge.

TIPS BOX

If you like the idea of using a scraper, but are not so happy about the sharpening procedure, then you will find that there are one or two nice little gizmos on the market that make the task easy and foolproof.

Sharpening a Scraper

The important thing about the scraper is not so much how it is used – this is very easily learned by trial and error – but rather how it is sharpened. If you have a close-up look at a scraper in action, you will see that it is the minute, turned-up edge of the burr that does the cutting. When the burr gets to be rounded, then the scraper fails to cut. To sharpen the scraper, set it in the vice and use a file to cut the edge down square. Next, hold the scraper edge-down on an oilstone, keeping it upright and at right angles to the stone, and systematically run it straight backwards and forwards until the filed edge is square, crisp and clean. Now, set the scraper flat-down on the stone and polish the slight burr as left by the honing. Lastly, set the scraper in the vice so that the edge is standing proud, then take a burnisher or any hardened, round-section tool, like the back of a round gouge, and run it repeatedly at an angle along the corner-edge so as to raise the burr. Repeat this procedure on both edges. If you have done it right, the edge will be "burnished and burred" or turned up at the corners.

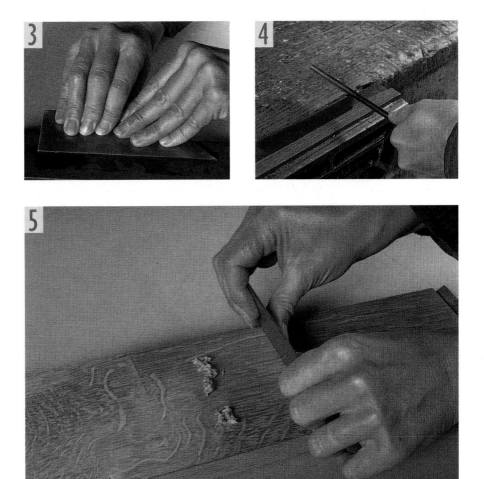

3 Burnish and remove the slight burr.

4 Run a hardened round-section tool as a burnisher along the edge to bring up the burr. Do this on both edges.

5 A well-tuned scraper will produce the best of all surfaces – many times smoother than a plane or sandpaper.

ABOVE: Bow the scraper with your thumb until it begins to "feel and bite".

SCRAPER PLANES

Handle

Scraper blade

Retaining screw

MADE IN
STANLEY
ENGLAND

Tension thumb screw

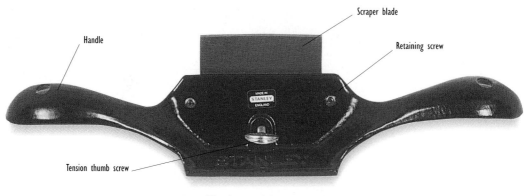

ABOVE: The design of the scraper plane means that it can be used for long periods without cramping or fatigue.

Known variously as a scraper plane, a scraper shave, a cabinet spokeshave scraper and one or two other names besides, this tool is designed to scrape and polish, as in cabinet work. Many woodworkers are so skilled at using the scraper plane that they go from using the smoothing plane straight through to using the scraper plane without the need for sanding. If you have a close-up look at a well-tuned scraper plane in action, you will see that it produces the finest paper-thin shavings, leaving a finish that is glass-smooth. The tool is held like a spokeshave or a plane, depending upon the design, and then run with the grain at a slight angle for a shearing cut. This is a tool that favours hard, dense wood.

BELOW: The scraper plane in action.

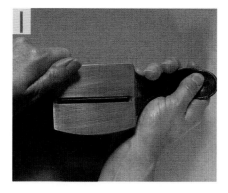

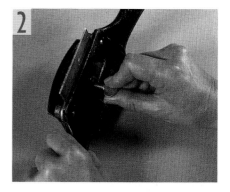

Using a Scraper Plane

1 Set the blade fair and square in the mouth so that it stands slightly proud, then tighten up the two outside thumbscrews.

2 Tighten up the central screw so that the blade bows.

3 Secure the workpiece, set the tool down so that the curved edge is leading the way, then make the first cut.

OTHER SCRAPER TOOLS

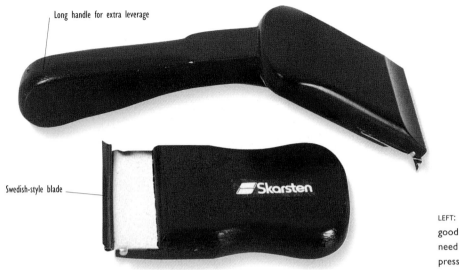

Long handle for extra leverage

Swedish-style blade

Skarsten

LEFT: Hook scrapers – a good design when you need to apply extra pressure.

ABOVE: The throw-away scraper is fitted with a blade and although designed to be used on the "push" stroke, it can also be used on the drag stroke.

Polypropylene handle

ABOVE: Carbide mini scraper with a triangular three-edged blade.

Double-edged tungsten carbide blade

ABOVE: Carbide universal scraper with 5 cm (2-in) long blade.

TIP BOX

If you are a beginner to woodwork, and you are looking only to stock your workshop with fine traditional tools, then a scraper plane is a must! Most new scrapers are many times more expensive than the old ones, so the best deal is to buy second-hand originals.

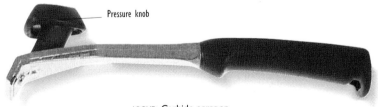

Pressure knob

ABOVE: Carbide scraper with pressure knob.

Assembly

Although the need to hold, secure and otherwise stabilize a piece of woodwork is crucial to woodworking success, it is surprising how many projects catastrophically fail and come to grief at the assembly stage. What usually happens is that the woodworker takes the various assembly and fastening techniques for granted – the nailing, gluing or whatever – to the extent that the workpiece splits, warps, stains or is otherwise less than perfect. At a time when there are many more sophisticated assembly techniques than ever before, it is most important that you keep up with current techniques.

SCREWDRIVERS

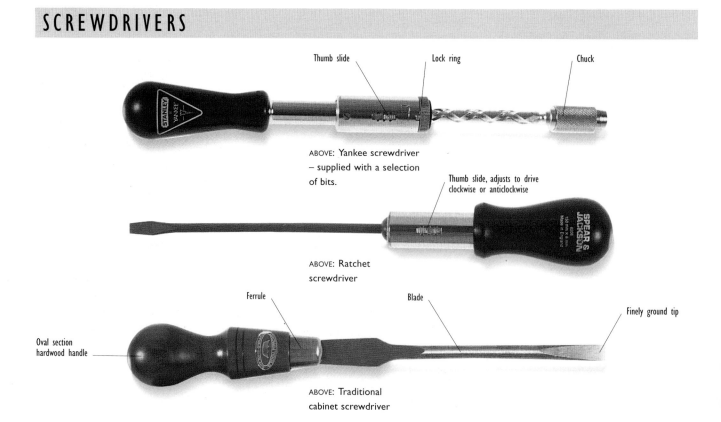

Thumb slide · Lock ring · Chuck

ABOVE: Yankee screwdriver – supplied with a selection of bits.

Thumb slide, adjusts to drive clockwise or anticlockwise

ABOVE: Ratchet screwdriver

Ferrule · Blade · Finely ground tip

Oval section hardwood handle

ABOVE: Traditional cabinet screwdriver

Though the screwdriver is one of those tools that gets to be used for just about everything from stirring paint to chiselling out mortises, it is nevertheless a tool that crucially affects the quality of the finish. Use the wrong screwdriver and the chances are that you will damage the screw or scratch your work or both.

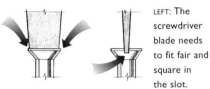

LEFT: The screwdriver blade needs to fit fair and square in the slot.

Screwdriver Type

For a screwdriver to successfully perform its task, the tip needs to fit the head of the screw, and the handle needs to fit your hand. Most woodworkers agree that you can't do better than the traditional "cabinet" pattern, with its oval- section wooden handle. However, there are currently so many screw types on the market –

ABOVE: The Yankee-type screwdriver – with its chuck and selection of bits – is a great all-round tool.

Phillips, pozidrive, red and prince, clutch, and Robertson, to name just a few – that a good option is to have a selection a cabinet pattern screwdrivers for the traditional slotted screws, and a spiral type "Yankee" screwdriver with its chuck and a selection of bits to do the rest. When you come to choose a screwdriver head to match the screw, then make sure that it is a good snug fit in the slot. It shouldn't be so wide that it projects at either side of the screw and scratches the workpiece, nor so narrow that it twists around on the spot and strips the head of the screw

FITTING BRASS SCREWS

1 Drill a small diameter pilot hole into the wood.

2 Follow the pilot hole up with a bit sized to fit the screw.

3 Use a countersink bit to sink a cone-shaped hole big enough to take the screw head.

4 Compare the head size with the countersink holes, then make adjustments as necessary.

5 Dip the screw in beeswax polish and drive it home.

TIPS BOX

If you have in mind to drive hundreds of screws or you have weak wrists or you just like power tools, then the power screwdriver is a good option. Don't try to cut costs by using an attachment in a power drill, it's much better to get yourself a dedicated tool, preferably one with its own independent power pack.

HAMMERS AND NAILING

Ash handle

Peen

Cheek

Neck

Bell

ABOVE: Warrington joiner's hammer – for general work.

ABOVE: Cross-peen hammer – for light work.

Tempered steel shaft

Claw

Blue vinyl grip

ESTWING

ABOVE: Claw hammer with solid one-piece integral handle, for general work.

Woodworkers need at least three hammers: a claw hammer, an Exeter or a Warrington cross-peen hammer, and a small cross-peen pin hammer. As with planes, there is a hammer for every task. And of course, there are hammers bad and hammers good. Though the hammer is one of those tools that is often abused or just simply taken for granted, a good hammer can make the difference between a job well done, and a job less than perfect. If you want a good hammer – a joy to use and a friend for life – then the following brief listing will help you in your choice.

BELOW: Hold the hammer by the end of the handle to achieve maximum leverage.

LEFT: Driving out the remains of a broken handle.

Claw Hammer

The claw hammer – usually called a carpenter's or joiner's hammer – is the hammer to use for driving large nails. Usually these hammers come in three weight sizes, a 450g (16-oz.), a 600g (20-oz.), and a 750g (24-oz). These hammers are characterized by having a hickory handle to absorb the shock of the blow, a striking face that is both hardened and polished, a head that is softer than the face, and a claw shape that enables the woodworker to draw out even the most awkward nails. If you have a choice, choose the socket-head type. As for handles – they're available in wood, steel, fibre glass

and other hybrids – most woodworkers prefer hickory. They claim that wood absorbs shock without being too springy.

Warrington Cross-Peen

The cross-peen Warrington pattern hammer has long been thought of as being the best tool for the cabinet maker. Coming in six weight sizes that range from 170g (6-oz) through to 450g (16-oz.), the Warrington hammer has a slender flat-ground peen for starting off the nails, and a flat-forged polished face for accurate driving.

Warrington Cross-Peen Pin Hammer

ABOVE: Securing a new handle with a wedge.

At 100g ($3\frac{1}{2}$oz.), the pin hammer is simply a lightweight version of the Warrington pattern with a much longer, more slender handle. If you plan to do a lot of small delicate tasks, such as picture framing, or maybe making small desktop toys, then this is the tool you want.

USING A PIN HAMMER

1 To tap a pin into a delicate bead, first locate the pin, then carefully tap it into place with the face of the hammer.

2 When you are happy with the pin location, turn the hammer over and use the tail of the hammer and a few well-placed blows to drive the pin home.

PULLING OUT NAILS WITH A CLAW HAMMER

1 To drive the nail in: hold the handle near its end, and bang the nail home with a few well-placed blows.

2 To remove the nail: ease the first centimetre or so out with the claw.

3 For extra leverage, use a block of waste to raise the head of the hammer well clear of the surface, then arc the hammer over so as to lever out the nail.

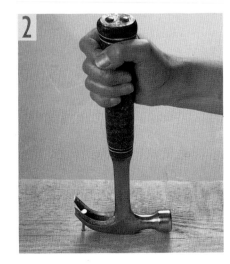

JOINT GLUING

Gluing Techniques

Most woodwork needs to be glued. Certainly there are all manner of dry joints that rely on nails, screws, dowels and various patent hardware, but the truth is that modern glues are so fast, easy to use, reliable and strong that gluing is a technique that needs to be mastered. But what glue to use? Do you want a user-friendly glue that allows you the option of disassembling the workpiece at some time in the future? Or do you want a fix that is forever – a bond that is stronger than the wood itself? The following selection guide will help you match your needs to the available choices.

Hide Glue (Hot)

An animal protein glue, hot hide glue requires a glue pot. It has fast tack, is transparent, not water resistant, non-toxic, can be sanded and is good for restoring antique furniture.

Hide Glue (Cold)

Also an animal protein glue, cold hide glue used straight from the tube/tin is a glue with slow tack. It is transparent, non-toxic, can be sanded, is slow setting and good for difficult assemblies.

Casein Glue

Made from milk, this glue must be mixed with cold water. It is opaque, non-toxic, good for cool working conditions and oily exotic woods.

White Glue

A PVA glue, this adhesive is made from petrochemicals. Used straight from the squeezy container, it is transparent, non-toxic and good for interior woodwork. White glue goes rubbery when sanded, but it is good for general do-it-yourself woodwork.

Yellow Glue

Also a PVA glue, yellow glue is similar to white glue. You can use it straight from the squeezy container. It offers fast tack, is almost transparent, non-toxic, can be sanded and is good for both indoor and outdoor use.

LEFT: To remove a dribble of glue: wait for the glue to become rubbery, then cut off the dribble with a sharp chisel.

Resin Glue

A mix-with-water powder glue, this adhesive is brown in colour. Be warned that it is toxic in its powder form. Resin glue tends to be brittle, but it sands well and is good for general use.

Dry Run Gluing

Having chosen your glue, and generally made sure you know all there is to know about mixing, setting time, precautions and all the rest, then comes the time for the dry run before the actual glue-up. This procedure involves you in doing everything except actually brushing on the glue. Start by choosing a clean, dust-free area in the workshop, somewhere that you can work without interruption. Make sure that the mating faces to be glued are clean and free from dust, and then put them together. If you need a mallet, then set it at the ready. Prepare scraps of clean wood to protect the workpiece from the clamps, and clamp up. Make decisions along the way as to whether or not you want throw-away containers, or clothes, or protective gloves, and set them out accordingly. And so you continue, from first to last, running through the procedure until the workpiece is clamped and complete. Finally, when you have run through the whole checklist and you are happy with the order of work, then you remove the clamps, set out the various elements of the workpiece and start gluing up for real.

RIGHT: Hold the boards together so that you can glue both edges at the same time.

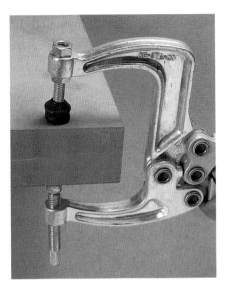

ABOVE: A set of aluminium scissor clamps with adjustable heads and rubber pads.

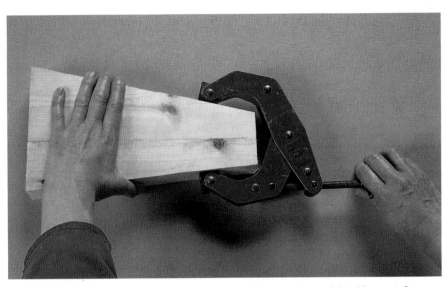

ABOVE: There are some very clever clamps on the market. This particular model is able to grip faces that are less than parallel – such as wedges.

ABOVE: This particular clamp can be tightened up without any twist-damage action.

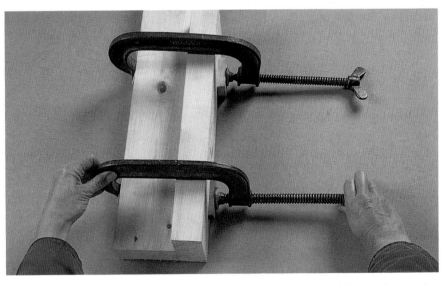

ABOVE: The damage caused by the twisting action of C-clamps can be negated by the use of scraps of wood known as "wasters" that are placed between the clamp and the workpiece.

ABOVE: Toggle clamps screwed to a base board make a good jig board.

TIPS BOX

If you have been generous with the glue, to the extent that a small amount oozes out, then best leave it to partially set before removing it with a knife or chisel. BE WARNED – if you wipe the glue ooze off with a cloth, then the glue will be pushed into the pores of the wood, and that area will resist the final wax, oil, stain or finish.

VENEERING

Veneering is the art and craft of gluing a thin sheet of exotic or precious wood to a common wood groundwork. The object of the exercise is to fool the eye into believing that the workpiece – say a table or screen – is made in its entirety from the precious wood. There are many reasons for veneering. For example, you can make a precious wood go further, create surface patterns and give the illusion that a piece of furniture is made from a particular wood, while, in fact, it would be structurally impossible to do so. For instance, it would be impossible to construct a piece of furniture from ebony, simply because it would be too heavy. And then again, while burr walnut is a wonderfully attractive wood, it is so brittle and unstable that it would fall to bits when machined in the round. Traditionally, the veneering technique involves heating up hide glue, coating the groundwork and/or the sheet of veneer with the hot liquid glue, bringing the two together, smoothing the veneer with a special weighted hammer and then variously pressing and clamping the veneer in place – before finally scraping, sanding and finishing.

Not so long ago, veneering was viewed more or less as a technique that primarily had to do with concealing poor workmanship. The current desire by the various "green" movements to conserve rare wood, has resulted in a popular revival of interest in veneering. What better way of protecting an endangered species than by making a little go a long way? All that said, if you are interested in using exotic species, you want to save money, and you want to minimize your usage of rare wood, then it logically follows that you need to learn about veneering techniques.

Heavy gauge nickel-plated copper inner pot

LEFT: Thermostatically controlled glue pot that does not require water.

Stainless steel rollers

Chamfered corners

ABOVE: J-type veneer roller.

Axle projection only on one side

ABOVE: Veneer hammer, used for pressing down veneers and squeezing out excess glue.

Rounded brass strip inset

Veneering with PVA Adhesive

Though traditionally veneering was a craft that had to do with complex presses, hot glue, tricky sheets of veneer that were liable to crack and curl and all manner of unpredictable difficult-to-manage techniques, the current interest in the craft has resulted in some exciting quick-and-easy methods. For example, there are adhesives that stick on impact without heat and pressure, and there are cold glues that can be used straight from squeezy containers. There are also thermoplastic glue-films, that can be pressed in place with a domestic hot iron, and so on. And then again, many of the difficulties that had to do with constructing a suitable substrate have been solved by the introduction of an incredibly stable man-made sheet material called medium-density fibreboard or simply MDF. And perhaps most interesting of all, there are now super-thin flexible veneers that come in rolls that can be handled with relative ease.

ABOVE: A veneering saw in action.

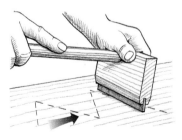

ABOVE: A veneering hammer in action.

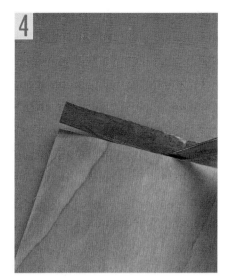

Using Flexible "Art" Veneer and PVA Adhesive

1 **Cutting to Size** – Having decided how you want the direction of the grain to run, use a metal straight edge and a craft knife to cut the veneer to size. Aim for a generous, all-round fit. Identify and label the best face of the veneer. Dampen the best face with water, so as to prevent curl.

2 **Applying the Glue** – Brush the PVA adhesive evenly on the substrate and on the mating surface of the veneer. Leave to dry.

3 **Hot Ironing** – When the PVA adhesive is completely dry, align the veneer on the groundwork and hold it in place with tabs of masking tape. Use a hot iron to press the veneer in place.

4 **Finishing** – Finally, trim back the edges of the veneer with the craft knife, then use the sandpaper to rub the whole works down to a smooth finish.

PLIERS

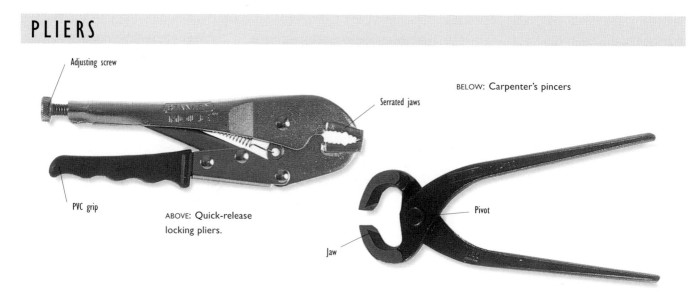

Adjusting screw

PVC grip

ABOVE: Quick-release
locking pliers.

Serrated jaws

BELOW: Carpenter's pincers

Jaw

Pivot

Woodworkers are forever needing to use pliers and grips for pulling out tacks, for holding tacks, for shaping wire, for making running repairs to tools, for straightening this and for bending that. You can't always know what type of pliers or grips you are going to need the next time around, but the following will give some idea of the options.

Pliers

A couple of pairs of well-made pliers are a must. Best get a large general purpose pair for all the heavy gripping, twisting, bending and cutting, and then get a pair of long-nosed pliers for working in tight corners and for extracting broken screws. As for quality, always go for the type described as "made from high quality carbon steel".

Pincers

Carpenter's pincers are one of those much used and abused tools that seem to have been around forever. With names like Tower pincers, French pattern pincers, boxed pincers and one or two other curious names besides, they are perfect for easing out bent and battered nails. To use the tool, first grip the nail in the jaws, and then the whole tool is rolled and pivoted on the outer jaw so that the tool becomes a very

efficient lever. As to the purpose of some of the outlandish knobs that some of these traditional pincers have at the end of the handles, who knows?

Mole Wrench

Wrenches of this type are so familiar that they hardly need describing. Perhaps enough to say that the clamping mechanism makes this tool extremely useful for all manner of gripping and twisting tasks. They are especially useful for gripping and holding circular objects like bolts and rods, and for extracting broken screws.

Nail Extractor

Nail extractors come in many shapes and sizes – some with wooden handles that look a bit like a screwdriver, and others made of black iron that look for all the world like a chicken's foot. Either way they

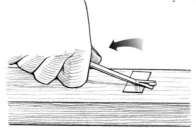

ABOVE: Using a nail extractor.

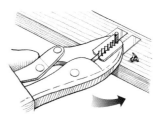

ABOVE: Using a pair of grips
to extract a broken screw.

are useful when you want to ease out a nail without using the claw hammer.

Screw Extractor

Though there are all manner of extractors, the simplest is rather like a plug cutter. In use, the tooth-ended tube is placed over the screw and given a couple of turns so that the stump of the screw is revealed. The screw is then gripped with a pair of long-nose pliers or a mole wrench and extracted.

Ajustable Wrench

A good quality adjustable wrench is the perfect tool for the woodworker who needs to deal with the occasional large nut and bolt, and yet doesn't want to go to the expense of purchasing a whole set of large-size open-ended wrenches. For example, a large wrench is needed on older style lathes to grip the drive shaft when the four-jaw chuck is unscrewed. And then again, it is

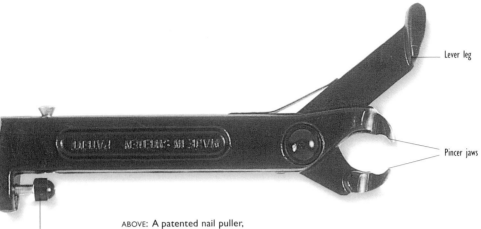

Lever leg

Pincer jaws

Hammer claw
location bolt

ABOVE: A patented nail puller,
designed to pull everything
from the smallest headless
tack to a 12.6cm (5-in) nail.

sometimes necessary to crawl under the
workbench and get a pair of pliers on the
coach bolts that secure the vice. All this
adds up to the fact that a good quality
wrench is a sound idea!

NOTE: if you want to use pliers on a shaft
without making marks, then it is best to
protect or pad the shaft with several winds
of masking tape.

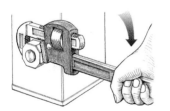

ABOVE: Adjustable wrench

ABOVE: Grip the nail so the rounded jaws of the
pincers are in contact with the workpiece.

ABOVE: Lever the pincers down and over so the
rounded jaws act as a fulcrum.

ABOVE: The split end of the handle is designed to
be used as a tack extractor.

Special Tools

Woodworkers have long been interested in special tools, meaning clever tools designed to get a particular task done faster, easier, at a lower cost or more precisely. With the revival of interest of hand tool techniques, there has been a revival of interest in a whole range of new and traditional special tools. If you are looking to increase your woodworking efficiency, then it might be worth your while to focus on special hand tool techniques.

THE DRAWER-LOCK CHISEL

The drawer-lock chisel is specifically designed to cut lock recesses in drawer fronts where the drawer is so shallow that the length of a regular chisel would bump into the back of the drawer. The cranked shape of the chisel enables the user to chop in the recess by tapping the back of the chisel with a hammer. It may not be a very exciting little tool, but it gets the job done.

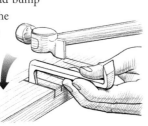

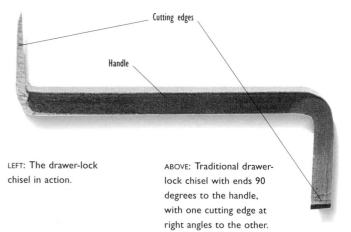

Cutting edges

Handle

LEFT: The drawer-lock chisel in action.

ABOVE: Traditional drawer-lock chisel with ends 90 degrees to the handle, with one cutting edge at right angles to the other.

THE NAILER PLANE

ABOVE: The nailer plane or chisel.

The nailer plane very nicely solves the problem of how to use nails without the heads and holes showing. The traditional solution is to use a chisel to pare up a shaving, to locate the nail or pin in the resultant recess and then to glue the little curl of wood back in place. A simple enough technique you might think, but what often happens is that the chisel slips or the shaving gets lost. The invisible nailer – more or less a copy of the old gauge chisel tool – solves the whole problem by lifting shavings of a regular thickness so that they become little hinged flaps. It's a foolproof tool, great if you like to have your nails hidden from view.

CORNERING TOOL

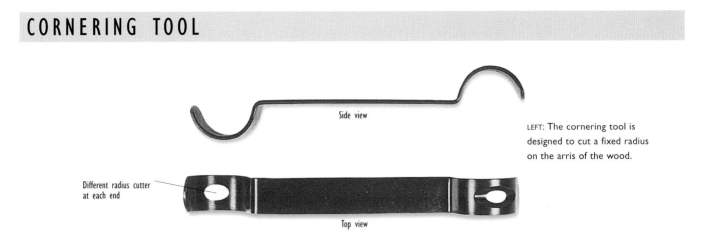

Side view

Different radius cutter
at each end

Top view

The cornering tool is designed to shave the arris down to a radius section. In function, it is very much like a small "hollow" plane, or you might say a moulding plane. Made of flat steel and about 15 cm (6 in) long and 1.75 cm (½ in) wide, there are several sizes, each designed to cut a specific radius – 16 mm (¹⁄₁₆ in), 32 mm (¹⁄₈ in), 48 mm(³⁄₁₆ in) and 64 mm (¼ in). The tool is laid on the arris of the wood – meaning on the sharp corner – and then it is pushed or pulled so the blade pares off a thin shaving. Repeated cuts are made until the corner is down to

ABOVE: Cornering tool.

the required radius. Though these tools are currently being manufactured again, old ones are relatively easily found in flea market stalls.

TIPS BOX

One might ask if it would be better to use a power router for rounding the arris or corners of the wood. The answer depends on how many corners you need to round! If you only want to tidy up the odd bit of work, then the hand tool is fine. But if you want to start some sort of quick production line for a number of pieces, then the power router is perhaps the best way to go.

THE CARVER'S BENCH SCREW

The carver's bench screw, also known simply as a carver's screw, is designed for clamping bulky lumps or blocks of wood to the bench. To use the traditional iron bench screw, first a pilot hole is drilled into the underside of the workpiece. The screw is then screwed into the hole until it is good and tight. Next the screw is passed down through a hole in the bench. Finally, the large wing nut is threaded onto the screw and tightened up until the whole works is held secure. With the traditional iron bench screws, the massive butterfly nut has square holes in the wings that allow the whole wing nut to be used as a wrench to tighten up the screw

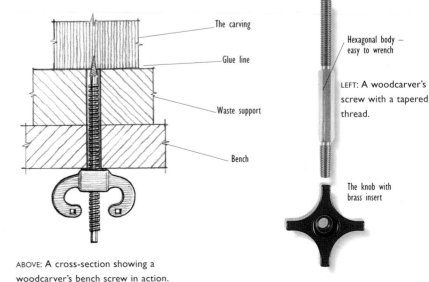

The carving

Glue line

Waste support

Bench

Hexagonal body –
easy to wrench

LEFT: A woodcarver's
screw with a tapered
thread.

The knob with
brass insert

ABOVE: A cross-section showing a
woodcarver's bench screw in action.

THE EDGE TRIMMER PLANE

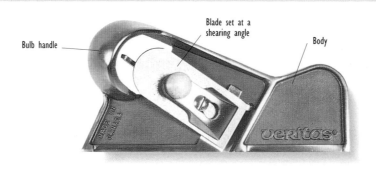

LEFT: The edge trimmer plane is used for making controlled cuts on the edge of boards to ensure that the edge is at right angles to the face.

The classic all-metal edge trimmer plane is the perfect follow-up tool to be used after the jointer plane. The board is set flat-down on the bench so that the edge to be worked is overhanging the top. The plane is set down on the board so that the vertical part of the sole is bearing hard up against the edge to be worked and then the stroke is made. As with most planes that have a fence, the whole success of the technique hinges on making sure that the fence is bearing hard up against the workpiece. In this instance, the fence and the sole are one and the same, with the cutting iron being set at a skewed angle in the integral sole-fence, so it is vital that both the horizontal and vertical parts of the L-section sole are hard against the wood. From plane to plane, the skewed 2.25–2.5-cm (⁷⁄₈–1-in)-wide cutting iron allows for precise trimming of boards that are to be used for close and accurate butt joints. Remember that the plane is designed to trim back to a finished 90-degree angle. It is much easier to tidy up an edge that cants back to an acute angle than it is to trim an edge that cants out to an obtuse angle. If you are working a board that has two good faces, then it will pay you to position the board so that the edge to be worked is slightly undercut.

THE COMPOUND MITRE SAW

Known variously as a compound mitre saw, a compound mitre box, a saw mitre-box and an adjustable mitre box, this is the best tool for woodworkers who are involved in cutting mitres. It is perfect for making picture frames and for cutting mouldings for panel, door and window surrounds. In essence, it is simply a mitre box with a built-in saw or at least a track for a saw. There are any number of slightly different designs, but with most the procedure is the same. The workpiece is set against a fence and clamped in place, the saw in its integral frame is swung around and set at the chosen angle, and then the saw is pushed backwards and forwards in its tracks. This tool wins on two counts: the angle of the cut is fixed and sure; and the saw blade is held at right angles to the face of the workpiece. All these features add up to a tool that takes the sweat and aggravation out of cutting mitres.

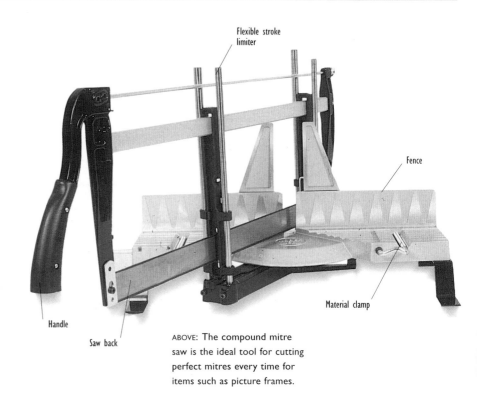

ABOVE: The compound mitre saw is the ideal tool for cutting perfect mitres every time for items such as picture frames.

THE MITRE TRIMMER

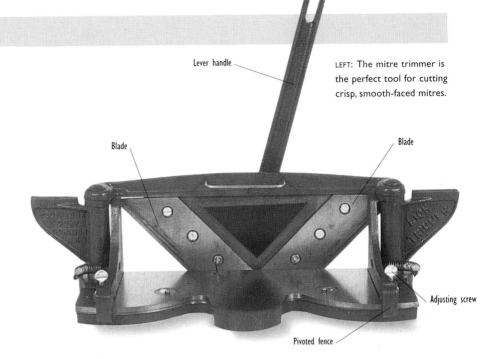

The mitre trimmer, known also as a mitre guillotine, is a machine that is dedicated to the single task of making accurate 90-degree and 45-degree cuts. If you have ever looked at the corner of a picture frame and wondered just how they achieve such a perfect finish, well this is the machine that does the job. To use the tool, the fence is set and locked at either 45 or 90 degrees. Then the wood is sawn slightly oversize and set hard up against the fence. Next, the arm of the machine is pulled down, so that the shearing action of the blade skims a thin shaving off the sawn face of the mitre. The shearing action produces a perfect butter-smooth finish every time.

Lever handle

LEFT: The mitre trimmer is the perfect tool for cutting crisp, smooth-faced mitres.

Blade

Blade

Adjusting screw

Pivoted fence

THE SPIRIT LEVEL

Do woodworkers need to use a level? Well, it really depends on whether or not you intend building in the items that you have made. For instance, you don't generally need to use a level to make a bookcase, but you most certainly do if you intend building the bookcase into a room.

Though there are all manner of level designs, they are all used to test either horizontal level, vertical plumb level or both. One end or other of the level is lifted until the bubble is on the line, and then the distance of lift is measured to ascertain how far the workpiece is off level.

ABOVE: Traditional level, with a rosewood body, a brass plate and brass-tipped ends. Dead level is achieved when the bubble is at the centre of the vial.

WOODTURNER'S CENTRE FINDER

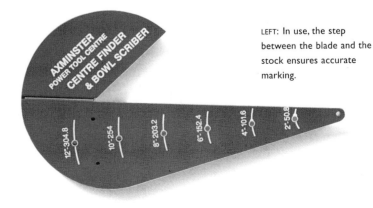

This little tool is designed to find the centre of a round blank. Simply set the tool on the end of the blank and draw a line, turn the tool slightly and draw another line and so on three or four times. The intersection of the lines pinpoints the centre. If you enjoy woodturning, then this is a handy tool.

LEFT: In use, the step between the blade and the stock ensures accurate marking.

Renovating Old Tools

The success of a technique depends to a great extent on the tools, so it is vital that you have good selection of quality tools. To this end, many woodworkers opt for working with old traditional hand tools, meaning tools that were made in the first half of this century. They claim that not only are such tools made to a higher standard when compared to modern hand tools, but better yet, they reckon that the shapes and designs of old tools are more user-friendly, with wooden handles and lots of good-to-hold curves. Be that as it may, it is a fact that good quality second-hand tools can easily be obtained at a fraction of the cost of new ones.

PLANES

Cleaning and Lapping a Metal Plane

You have purchased a second-hand plane, taken it apart and checked the frog, the cutting iron and all the moving parts, and they all look fine. The only thing is, the sole and sides are scratched and scruffy. Here's what you do: disassemble the plane, unscrew the wooden knob and the tote or handle so that you are left with the cast body. Clean off the resin and sawdust with white spirit. If it is slightly rusty or maybe paint-splattered, dip a wad of fine grade steel wool in some light oil and clean the metal down to a bright finish. Stick a sheet of fine grade wet-and-dry silicon carbide abrasive paper grit-side-up to a perfectly flat surface. You are now ready for the procedure know as "lapping". First, take a felt-tip marker or some machinist's layout dye, either black or blue, and paint the sole and the cheeks of the plane. Colour them all over. Then set the sole down on the paper and run it backwards and forwards until the colour has been removed and the whole surface is clean and shiny. Repeat the procedure for the two cheeks.

Lapping the Plane

1 Use a felt tip pen to colour the entire surface of the sole of the plane

2 Run the plane repeatedly over the fine grade carbide paper until all the colour has been removed.

WOODCARVING TOOLS

Renovating Woodcarving Gouges

While a quick flick through a current tool catalogue will show you that woodcarving gouges are very expensive, a visit to the average flea market will show you that gouges can be had for pennies. Now, the second-hand gouge might well be in a mess, but no matter, it can be brought back to life. Start by wiping the blade with beeswax polish and rubbing it down with the finest grade wire wool. Do both the inside and outside curves. Square the end of the blade off on an oilstone – not too much, just enough to remove the nicks. Hold the gouge up to the light and hone the bevel to a high-shine finish. Finally, use metal polish to clean the brass ferrule and wax polish the handle.

ABOVE: The same gouge before and after it has been cleaned and tuned.

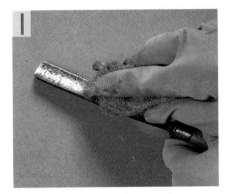

Cleaning the Gouge

1 Wipe the gouge with beeswax and use fine grade wire wool to polish the steel to a high shine.

2 Use a slip to swiftly bring the cutting bevel to a clean edge, then hone the bevel to the required angle.

3 Use a shaped slip to remove the burr from the inside of the blade.

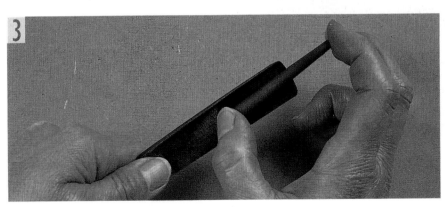

SAWS

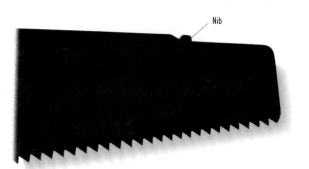

Nib

LEFT: The mysterious nib
– as seen on classic saws.

RIGHT: A brass back and
skewed blade indicate that
the saw is a quality tool.

Brass back

The Nibbed Toe Saw

The function of the small notch or "nib", as found on the back of some older saws is something of a mystery. Some woodworkers claim that it is used to start the cut, others say that it has to do with the wooden strip that some woodworkers tied over the teeth and yet others maintain it is the last vestige of a decorative feature that echoes back to early eighteenth century-

saws. All that said, if you see such a nib when you are searching around for a second-hand saw, then you can at least be pretty certain that the saw is a top quality item that is well worth renovating.

The Tapered Brass Back

If, when you are searching through the "bargain" box at a flea market, you find a back saw with a brass spine, a blade that is

tapered along its length and has about 12 points to 2.55cm (1 in), then you can be reasonably certain that it is a "superior" quality carcase saw. As the name suggests, saws of this type and character were used to cut the joints on the frames of pieces of furniture like dressers. If you find such a saw, then hang on tightly, quietly hand over your money and walk away.

HANDLES

BELOW: A well-shaped handle
is a joy to the eye and a
pleasure to hold.

Closed handle set at
correct angle to blade

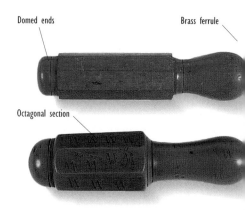

Comfortable to hold
with rounded, good-
to-look at curves

Superior Handles

As a general rule, the older the saw, then the fancier and more detailed the handle and the better quality the saw. And, of course, it doesn't stop there. If the handle feels good, then the whole sawing procedure becomes that much more pleasuresome.

Gouge Handles

One of the best guides as to the quality of an old gouge is the shape and substance of the handle. Although old gouge handles were variously made from fruitwood, beech, rosewood, ebony and mahogany, the superior quality handles were made from boxwood. In the old catalogues the most expensive gouges had handles described as "turned octagon box" – meaning they were

turned on the lathe from an octagonal section of boxwood. Another little clue as to quality was that the owners often spent time stamping their initials on the handle.

Domed ends

Brass ferrule

Octagonal section

ABOVE: The octagonal handle is
comfortable and easy to grip and
will not roll off the bench top.

CHISELS

ABOVE: Flat-backed pattern

ABOVE: Mortise chisel.

Selecting Chisels

Just about the first thing you will see when you start raking through the bargain box are old chisels. Don't worry too much about the handles, because they can be replaced, but rather concentrate your attention on the length and quality of the blade. First and foremost, see if you can find a name. Best go for chisels made in Britain or America. Having selected named British and American chisels, then weed out anything that looks to be bent, broken, burnt, deeply pitted with rust or in any way cracked. When you have selected your chisels, then fit them with handles and grind, hone and polish the bevels as already described.

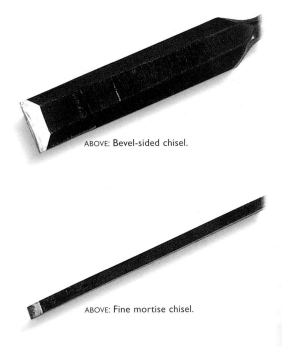

ABOVE: Bevel-sided chisel.

ABOVE: Fine mortise chisel.

DRILL BITS

Expanding Bits

Of all the old tools that can be found in junk shops and flea markets, the best bargain-buys of all time have surely got to be expanding bits. For example, while a new 7.5-cm (3-in) expanding bit is one of the most expensive items in the hand tool catalogue, old expanding bits of the same size can easily be had for a handful of loose change. That said, just make sure when you are checking over second-hand expanding bits that the lead screw, the cutting spur and lip, and the sliding track are intact. Undo the main fixing screw and move the expanding blade along the track. If all is well, it should be a nice sliding fit. While you are at it see if you can find any loose blades. Some types of expanding bits were sold with additional blades.

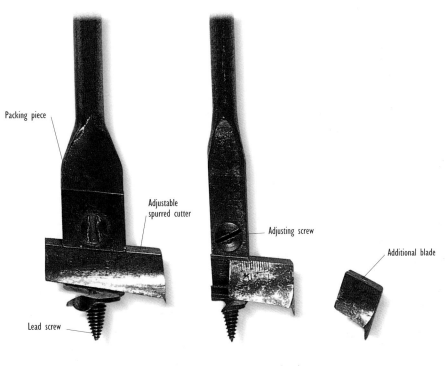

Packing piece

Adjustable
spurred cutter

Lead screw

Adjusting screw

Additional blade

ABOVE: A large size
expanding bit.

ABOVE: An expanding bit
with a spare small-size blade.

Wood Glossary

Trees are the biggest, most long-lived of all organisms. Their forests cover more than a quarter of the world's land surface. And like all living things, trees vary in size, colour and character. From species to species, some trees yield boards more than 2m (6ft) in width, while other trees give us woods that are variously hard textured, soft, close grained, oily, good to work, almost impossible to cut, toxic and so on. It is vital that you choose a wood that is appropriate to your needs.

Australian Blackwood

(Acacia melanoxylon)

Also known as Australian black wattle, or simply as wattle, this is a heavy, dense, straight-grained, very attractive, pale to reddish black wood. It is much in demand for prestigious interiors such as bank fixtures and quality furniture. It works to a crisp finish, takes a good polish and is really good for small ornamental turning and details.(S. Amer., Afr., Ind., Austr.)

Maple

(Acer spp.)

Known also as rock maple, sugar maple, field maple and one or two other names besides, this is creamy-coloured wood with a hard, close grain. It's important to note that although "soft maple" has many cross-over characteristics, it is generally softer and weaker than rock maple. Although it is relatively difficult to work, it does cut and carve to a wonderful sharp finish. (Can., U.S.A.)

Chestnut — Horse

(Aesculus hippocastanum)

A white to yellow-brown wood, with a fine grain and a uniform texture, traditionally used as a substitute for holly for furniture, carving, dairy utensils and for all manner of uses where a clean, odourless, white wood is preferred. If you enjoy making small turned items or you want to dye veneers, then this a good option. (U.S.A., U.K., Euro., China, Jap.)

Kauri Pine

(Agathis spp.)

Known in New Zealand as "King of the Trees", this is a straight-grained, white-pink to red-brown wood – very much like parana pine. This wood is used for everything from top grade furniture to boxes and crates. The wood is considered to be especially good for building small boats, for cabin work and decking. (N.Z., Austra.)

'Parana Pine' (S)

(Araucaria angustifolia)

This wood is not a true pine, but like pine, it is easy to work. It is straight grained, attractively honey coloured and has very little evidence of growth rings. Its main use is for internal joinery, such as staircases, drawers and furniture and it is often sliced for decorative veneers. (S. Amer.)

Pau Marfim

(Balfourodendron riedelianum)

A pale creamy yellow, fine-textured, straight-grained, featureless wood that was traditionally used for rulers, floors, shoe lasts and marquetry. It is a good wood for general furniture making. (U.S.A., S. Amer.)

Birch

(Betula spp.)

Known variously around the world as yellow birch, paper birch, European birch and many names besides. From country to country, birch is a pale cream to brown. A strong and stable hardwood, birch is traditionally used for making chairs and small turned items like brushes and bobbins. If you are interested in using plywood to make toys, then birch ply is your best bet. (Can., Euro., U.K.)

Boxwood

(Buxus sempervirens)

A very hard, dense-grained, pale yellow-cream hardwood. Boxwood was used by engravers for their blocks, and by turners for small items like chess pieces and pill pots. For small details like handles and knobs, boxwood is a good choice. However, it is very difficult to work with a plane. It works to a hard, high-shine finish like cream–yellow ivory. (Asia, Euro. U.K.)

Hickory

(Carya spp.)

Also known as pignut hickory, mockernut hickory and pecan hickory. With a grey-white colour and a rather ragged but straight grain, this wood is tough, and very difficult to work. It is the perfect wood for items that need a mix of strength and straight lengths such as chair legs. (Can., U.S.A., C. Amer.)

Chestnut — Sweet

(Castanea sativa)

A brown hardwood – very much like English oak in that the grain is firm and compact. It cuts, works and carves well. This wood is quite different from horse chestnut, which is a different species. Traditionally used for coffins, fence posts, gates, beams. (Euro., U.K., N. Afr., Asia)

Cedar — South American

(Cedrela mexicana)

Very much like mahogany, the only pronounced difference being the fragrant odour and the tendency to split. Used for making boxes, this is a good wood for boat building and furniture. It does tend to blunt the tools. (C. and S. U.S.A.)

Cedar — True

(Cedrus libani)

Named variously as the "true" cedar or the Mount Lebanon Cedar, this is the wood of Biblical fame that was used to build King Solomon's temple. It is brown, with a strong odour. Traditionally used for interior joinery and for furniture. If you have it in mind to build a chest, then this is a good choice. (N. Afr., Ind.)

Pencil Cedar

(Cupressaceae)

A soft, straight-grained wood with a fine, even texture, pencil cedar is used for making slats for lead pencils. It is also used for furniture, joinery, carpentry and for making cigar boxes. Because of its fragrant scent, it is popular for linen chests and for interior furniture linings. (Can., U.S.A.)

Satinwood — West Indian

(Chloroxylon swietenia)

A cream to golden-yellow wood, with a wavy grain and a fine, even texture. Used traditionally in the eighteenth century for furniture – Adam, Sheraton and Hepplewhite – it is now used primarily in furniture restoration. If you are looking to make small pieces of fine furniture, then it is still a good choice. (U.S.A., Jamaica)

Rosewood — Honduras

(Dalbergia spp.)

Also called Brazilian rosewood, this wood is a brilliant gold-to-brown chocolate colour, with a coarse texture and a grain that ranges from straight to wavy. Oily to the touch, rosewoods are valued as superior furniture wood and as a veneer. (C. & S. Amer.)

Jelutong

(Dyera costulata)

A pale cream-coloured wood, with a straight grain and a bland texture. Although a good wood for beginners to woodcarving to try, some people claim that the fine dust makes them sneeze. Best to go for carvings that require a minimum of sanding with lots of gouge-mark texturing. (Malaysia, Indon.)

Sapele

(Entandrophragma cylindricum)

A pale yellow to salmon-pink wood, with a straight grain and a fairly coarse texture, used primarily for shop fittings, doors and panels. The straight grain characteristics make this a good wood for pieces of special furniture. (Afr.)

Beech

(Fagus sylvatica or *Fagus grandifolia)*

A heavy, strong hardwood, with yellowish sapwood and reddish heartwood. Was and still is used for indoor work – furniture, tool handles, toys and the like. The even grain and texture makes this an excellent wood for planing and jointing. It works to a very smooth, hard, rather bland finish. (Austr., Can., Euro., Jap., N.Z., U.K., U.S.A)

Ash

(Fraxinus excelsior or *Fraxinus americana)*

A long-grained, tough, grey to red-brown hardwood traditionally used for tool handles, chair legs, agricultural implements, baseball bats and items that needed to be steam bent. Although ash is extremely hard to work, the resultant pieces of woodwork are both attractive and long lasting. The European and American varieties have very similar characteristics. (U.K., Can., U.S.A.)

Holly

(Ilex opaca and *Ilex aquifolium)*

Instantly recognizable as a growing tree, holly is characterized by being smooth, close-grained and white in colour – the whitest wood available. If the logwood is left to weather, it swiftly fades to a dull grey. Traditionally used in marquetry as a dyed substitute for other more exotic woods. This is a good wood for turning and carving. (Euro., U.K., U.S.A., China)

Walnut – European

(Juglans regia)

A grey to brown wood with a wavy grain and a coarse texture, used in times past for furniture, shop fittings and gun stocks. If you want to use walnut and still cut costs, then you could go for walnut veneers. Many woodworkers consider European walnut to be a better option that the American variety. (U.S.A., U.K., Euro., Asia, China)

Red Cedar

(Juniperus virginiana)

A reddish-brown, straight-grained hardwood with a strong fragrant aroma used traditionally for furniture, cigar boxes, ship interiors and coffins. The true pencil cedar is easy to plane and carve. The aroma makes this wood suitable for hope chests. (U.K., U.S.A, Can.)

Mahogany – African

(Khaya spp.)

Reddish brown in colour, with a straight but rather loose grain, "African mahogany" covers all the trees of the Khaya species. Though traditionally used for furniture and high-class interiors, there is now a shift in favour of using it in the form of thin veneers. Concerned woodworkers now consider that the overuse of mahogany needs to be discouraged. (Afr.)

Larch

(Larix europoea & decidua)

A softwood that is white–pink in colour, straight grained, resinous and even textured. The wood has been used for just about everything from pit props to bridge pilings, but is best used where there is a need for durability. It is difficult to work and carve, but the end result shows exciting grain. (Euro., U.K., U.S.A., Russia, China)

American Red Gum

(Liquidambar styraciflua)

The heartwood, known in the U.S. as sweet or red gum and in the U.K. as satin walnut, varies from pink-brown to a deeper red-brown often with darker streaks. The grain is irregular, with a fine uniform texture and a satin-sheen lustre, making it popular for furniture, interior trim, and panelling. Unless quarter-sawn the wood may warp or shrink if not dried properly. (U.S.A., Mex.)

Tulip Poplar

(Liriodendron tulipifera)

Known around the world as American whitewood, yellow poplar, canary whitewood, and tulip whitewood this creamy-white to pink-white hardwood has a fine, uniform texture and a satin-sheen lustre. It was used for such items as doors, trim, joinery and the like. It works to a good sharp finish and takes well to both stain and polish. (Can., U.S.A.)

Norway Spruce

(Picea abies)

Known also as European white wood and European spruce, this pale yellow to brown wood is straight grained and even textured with few knots and twists. It is used for interior framing, crates and pallets, and in the making of musical instruments. If you want to try some low-cost woodwork, carving or joinery, then this is a good choice. (U.K., Euro., Russia)

Pine — Western White

(Pinus monticola)

Known also as white pine and Idaho white pine, this wood is very similar in character to yellow pine. If you want to make a large project, then it might be as well to try with a small sample – just to see if your choice has the properties you seek. This wood is a good general all-round choice. (Can., U.S.A., U.K.)

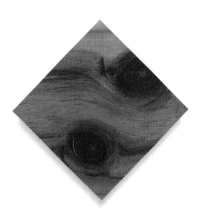

Pine — Ponderosa

(Pinus ponderosa)

A pale yellow to reddish-orange brown wood with an even texture and straight grain. It's a really good wood for kitchen and workshop furniture, and for general woodwork. It cuts to a sharp finish and takes both varnish and paint. (Can., U.S.A., Afr., Austr.)

Pine — Pitchpine

(Pinus rigida)

Sometimes confused with Ponderosa pine and western white, and also known variously as yellow pine, Quebec pine and long leaf pine. This heavily-grained wood, with alternate streaks of cream and brown, is straight grained, coarse in texture with a high resin content. In former times this wood was used for chapel pews and furniture. (U.S.A.)

Cottonwood — Poplar

(Populus deltoides)

Also known as Eastern cottonwood, swamp cottonwood, black cottonwood or simply as poplar, this wood is a greyish white, hard-wearing, straight-grained wood traditionally used for the whole gamut of woodworking activities. It's also known as poplar. Works to a slightly fluffy finish – the tools need to be sharp and thin-edged. (Can., U.S.A., U.K., Euro., China)

Cherry

(Europe Prunus avium –
USA Prunus serotina)

Known as European cherry, gean, mazzard, black cherry, and cabinet cherry, this is a creamy pink-to-brown, fine-textured, straight-grained wood – perfect for hand tool work. Cherry works to a sharp, high-shine finish, but tends to blunt the cutting tools. (U.S.A., Euro., U.K., China)

Fir — Douglas

(Pseudotsuga menziesii)

Known also as Columbian pine, red fir, Oregon pine and other names besides, it is a reddish-brown, straightgrained wood. In long lengths it is used traditionally for bridges, masts, pit props and residential construction. It is a good wood for common interior joinery. Although difficult to work, it has an exciting grain pattern. (Can., U.S.A., U.K., N.Z., Austr.)

Pear

(Pyrus communis)

A pale, apricot, pink-brown, fine-textured, straight-grained wood. Traditionally used as a fancy wood for small decorative items, it is particularly good for turning and carving. (U.K., Euro.)

Oak – White

(Quercus alba)

Known as English oak, European oak and American white oak, this is the wood of legend. It was made into ships and churches and carvings and caskets, where there was a need for massive strength and age-long durability. It is light tan to red-brown in colour with a straight, coarse grain. (Can., U.S.A., U.K., Euro., Jap.)

Oak American

(Quercus rubra)

Known usually as American red oak, this wood is similar to European oak in many respects – the biscuit to pink-brown colour and the straight, coarse grain – but while this wood is very good for interior work, it is totally unsuitable for exterior work. If you want to go for oak for furniture, then this is a good option. (Can., U.S.A.)

Willow

(Salix spp.)

A cream white-pink wood known around the world as white willow, common willow, crack willow and black willow. This wood was used for making cricket bats and everything from clogs, flooring and toys to automobile frames, brake blocks and fruit baskets. If you are looking for a good safe wood for making toys, then this is a good choice. (U.S.A., U.K., Euro., China)

African Pterygota

(Sterculiaceae)

This is a creamy-white wood with a grey tint and a shallowly interlocked grain that works easily with either hand or machine tools. Pterygota is used for furniture fitments, joinery and carpentry, boxes, crates and pallets. It is also sliced for decorative veneers, that need careful handling as they are rather brittle. (Africa)

Mahogany – American

(Swietenia spp.)

Known as Cuban or Spanish mahogany, this wood is yellowish-white through to red-brown, with straight grain, and a close relatively uniform texture. Mahogany is the traditional choice for furniture and interiors. Because mahogany is an endangered species, woodworkers are being encouraged to use look-alike alternatives. (C. Amer., S. Amer.)

Yew

(Taxus baccata)

Known also as common yew, English yew and European yew, this is orange to cream-brown, with a dense and straight grain. In England, yew has long been thought of as having special magic powers – good for such things as longbows and doors that are able to ward off the evil eye. (Euro.)

Basswood

(Tilia americana or Tilia glabra)

Almost identical in character to English lime. Pale cream-yellow in colour, it is very easy to work – especially to carve. It was used traditionally for general joinery and for the workings of pianos. If you want to try your hand at carving or sculpted furniture details, then this is a good wood. (Can., U.S.A.)

Lime – Linden & Basswood

(Tilia vulgaris)

Known also as linden and basswood, this wood has a close, straight grain, a pale butter colour and a smooth, even texture. Lime is considered to be the best wood for fine detail carving. While lime, linden and basswood are thought of as being one and the same, they are in fact a closely related but different species. (Euro., U.K., U.S.A., Can., Jap.)

Elm – American

(Ulmus americana or Ulmus thomasi)

A light to reddish brown wood with a straight grain and a slightly coarse texture. Traditionally used for ship building, wheel hubs and for agricultural implements. A good wood where you want a mix of lengths, strength and good bending qualities. (Can., U.S.A., Euro., N. Afri., Ind., China)

Elm – European

(Ulmus procera)

Also known as English elm, red elm, nave elm and coffin elm. It is strong, straight-grained and very durable. It was used and much valued for large roof spans, and wet conditions. It was also used for chairs, ladders, vehicle bodies and the like. Wych elm, a deviant, has a beautiful green tinge to the grain. (U.K., Euro., U.S.A., Jap.)

Index

CREDITS

Axminster Powertool Centre, Chard Street, Axminster, Devon: *pages 9, 18, 19, 20,*
21, 22, 23, 24, 26, 27, 28, 32, 34, 36, 40, 42, 44, 467, 47, 48, 50, 52, 53, 55, 56, 57, 58,
60, 61, 64, 65, 68, 70, 72, 78, 80, 82, 84, 85, 87, 88, 98, 100, 102, 104, 105, 106, 108,
109, 110, 111, 112, 114, 116, 118, 122, 124, 126 and 128.

Martin and Elders, Catharine Place, Bath, Avon: *pages 11, 66 and 67.*

All other photographs are the copyright of Quarto Publishing.

The following kindly loaned items for use in photography:
Ross Fuller *(carved green man mask, page 62)* and Peter Clothier *(carved cat, page 63.)*